ECONOMICS OF NATURAL RESOURCES IN INDIA

ECONOMICS OF NATURAL RESOURCES IN INDIA

G. PANNERSELVAM

ABHIJEET PUBLICATIONS
DELHI 110094

ABHIJEET PUBLICATIONS
2/46 Tukhmeerpur Extension
Delhi-110 094
Phone: 011-22960492, 65698474
E-mail: abhijeetpublication@gmail.com

ECONOMICS OF NATURAL RESOURCES IN INDIA

First Published 2008

ISBN 978-81-89886-97-4

PRINTED IN INDIA

Published by J.K. Singh for Abhijeet Publications, Delhi-110 094, Lasertypeset by Gaurav Graphics, New Delhi and Printed at Himanshu Printers, Delhi.

Dedicated To
My Beloved Parents

M. GOVINDHASAMY
&
NAGAMMAL

Preface

Natural Resources are the assets and boon to a country. It should be preserved in a well planned and sustainable manner. If we want to achieve sustainable growth. We must use it in a very scare manner. In the world level, India is a rich country, but Indians are poor. What is the reason? Because of the underutilization and mis utilization of natural resources.

If we utilize all the resources in an efficient manner India in near future will be emerging as the most biggest powerful ration in the whole world, in contrary, Japan is a poor country, but Japanese are rich, the reason is very well known.

This book tries to give a spatio-temporal analysis of the usage of natural resources.

To thank profusely scholars and authorities is a pleasure indeed.

I am greatly indebted to Dr.A.Arunachalam, M.A.,M.Phil.,M.L., Ph.D., M.B.A., Chairman and Correspondent of Adaikalamatha College, Vallam, Thanjavur.

I owe my sincere thanks to respected Principal Dr. R. KATHIAN, M. Com., M.Phil., Ph.D., for his timely help.

I feel happy to thank my Father-in-Law, Mother-in-Law, Brother, Sister and Daughter without their constant pressure and co-operation.

I am thankful to Abhijeet Publications New Delhi for their Interest and co-operation in publishing this book.

I do not claim that could cover all the aspects of the natural resources management within the limited space, but I firmly believe that this book will be very useful to all concerned.

G. PANNEERSELVAM
Thanjavur
May 2008

Contents

1

Natural Resources Scenario in India

Resources: Technologies and Truths

The complexity and contentiousness of the political economy of natural resources has been reiterated by the war in Iraq. Many key aspects of the US invasion can be analysed in terms of empire [Anderson 2002] and capitalist control over a critical resource like oil. Yet, these explanations do not exhaust either what is at stake or the form that conflicts around natural resources take. An approach that focuses on the economy of extraction is a necessary but not sufficient condition for understanding oil politics. A regime of extraction has other dimensions that are as constitutive of its meaning and power. Resource extraction is part of a regime of rule involving technologies, rationalities and institutions, made intelligible by regimes of truth that organise understanding and experience [Rose 1999]. These hegemonic truths are challenged and struggled over through cultural politics. In this introduction, I make a case for using cultural politics as an approach that enables a more insightful analysis of the significance of natural resources in contemporary life. The technologies of rule that develop around natural resources have most often been studied in terms of the imperial quest for stable regimes of extraction [Ludden 1992]. Wars of conquest and 'pacification' are followed by occupation and the coerced . rearrangement of relations of rule, production and exchange. Yet, profit —the economic calculus of private benefit—cannot be separated from passionate attachment to more lofty ideals. In the Iraqi case, as in other colonial schemes, the violence of extraction is tied to ideas of improvement, almost echoing Mill's declaration that "Despotism is the legitimate mode of government in dealing with barbarians, provided the end be their improvement". Thus, US military occupation is presented as a way to further the welfare of ordinary Iraqis through improved management of their polity and economy. This conceit is underwritten by a key imperial ideology: stewardship [Cowen and Shenton 1996], the notion that the 'more civilised' know best how to run the lives of subordinate peoples [Mehta 1999]. Ideas of improvement, predicated on liberalism's constructions of cultural difference, inform contemporary discourses of development—the imperative to efficiently maximise resource use, a goal best directed by technocratic experts, who lead the less-educated towards an enlightened, prosperous future.

Constructing stable regimes of extraction thus requires not just brute force, but also the mobilisation of 'consensus' such that people be willing participants. Official narratives frame the 'problem' in ways that legitimise particular forms of action. Trying to dress up domination as hegemony, the US administration and media titled their project 'Operation Iraqi Freedom', where freedom was understood as an end universally desired. Terrorism was presented as the enemy of all. Saddam Hussein was demonised as a monster whose overthrow would restore democracy and capitalist business-as-usual. To the extent that Americans and others around the world acceded to these representations, the campaign worked. Much has been written on the manufacture of consent for imperialist projects.3 I will not recapitulate those discussions except to highlight the connections they draw between imperialism and culture [Said 1993], connections that are made less often in debates about natural resources. If the war in Iraq was about oil, as it indeed was, it was also about freedom and terror, Arab nationalism and Christian fervour. One is no less real than the other; all have consequential effects. Appreciating the inseparability of the material and the symbolic dimensions of the conflict helps us understand that the political economy of a natural resource is meaningful only through the wider networks of cultural politics in which it is embedded.

At the same time, one must also appreciate the biophysical qualities of the resource. Oil has particular characteristics that necessitate specific forms of centralised, capital-intensive technologies of extraction that tend towards state control [Watts 2001]. Hence Iraqi oil could not be appropriated by Americans without deposing the Iraqi government. Then there is the strategic importance of oil within industrialism. For all the assertions by the Bush administration that the conflict was not about oil, critics pithily pointed out that if Iraq's major export was cauliflower, its political regime would not attract quite the same degree of concern. Each resource has distinctive use values that emerge in relation to particular modes of production. Petroleum in the present involves geopolitical formations like nation states [Coronil 1997], armies, firms and research establishments that make up the military-industrial complex, those who work to process and distribute oil and the billions of consumers who use it in one form or another. It also affects the fate of those who live in the areas where it is produced, both humans and other species. 'What is called nature or the material world moves... in and out of human forms, or occurs as arrangements... that are social as well as natural, technical as well as material' [Mitchell 2002: 52].

Political Ecology and Cultural Politics

The cultural politics approach to natural resources attempts to displace some of the assumptions that govern political ecology, the conceptual rubric under which extensive research has been conducted in India and abroad. Political ecology's great strength has been its unwavering focus on issues of social equality and justice at stake in conflicts over natural resources. This rich literature has examined social movements large and small that bring together diverse and distant social groups, address transnational audiences and use international and national regulatory and judicial institutions to defend threatened livelihoods against the incursions of state-led extractive development. However, while asymmetries of power are clearly identified as crucial in political ecology's analysis, they tend to be viewed through the binaries of civil society versus state, 'virtuous peasants' versus 'vicious states'. It is often assumed that the 'state' and 'communities' are separate, autonomous entities with self-evident interests that are clearly opposed. Critiques of such assumptions are now commonplace within anthropology and, even in studies of resource conflicts, more complex representations are beginning to gain ground. Thus a continued fondness for singular narratives to explain natural resource struggles is inexplicable. Such an analytical frame, I would argue, takes at face value the simplified political representations that social movements must generate in order to cohere. Yet this uncritical reproduction of claims, often intended as a gesture of solidarity, ignores the difficult, creative work of constructing political identities, forging alliances and transcending differences. In doing so, political ecology may not only fail to offer much analytical purchase, but may also be complicit in the continued political marginalisation of those excluded by dominant narratives of environmental movements. Collective representations created by activists, circulated and endorsed by academics, can have consequential effects.

Identities and interests are mutually formed through the contingent, lived experience of "situated cultural practices and sedimented histories of people and place" [Moore 1999: 658]. This messy process creates contradictions as subjects are formed within multiple fields of power. The adivasi fighting against displacement in the Narmada valley is simultaneously a tribal, a farmer, a collector of forest produce, a woman, a mother, a consumer of manufactured goods like fertilisers and saris, a worker on state drought-relief projects, in debt to a moneylender, a migrant, an anti-dam activist, a devout member of the Gayatri parivar, a panchayat leader, a voter in state and national elections, and so much more. These criss-crossing affiliations are not only intrinsic to how people live their quotidian lives, they are immensely consequential for shaping collective action. However, political ecology tends to assume that cultural identities are preformed, derived directly from an objective set of interests based on shared locations in terms of class, gender or ethnicity that challenge nationalism and/or capitalism.

Political ecology has also assumed that the primary significance of natural resources resides in their material use value. A forest becomes a bone of contention because its trees represent timber, fodder or fuel, material values desired by different social groups. Cultural politics suggests that natural resources have value within a larger economy of signification which crucially shapes their modes of appropriation. They are also resources for collective representations that exceed the concern with immediate material use. This 'social life of things' is well-illustrated in David Mosse's study of village water tanks in Tamil Nadu where dalits mobilised for representation in the association that managed these bodies [Mosse 2003: 279-282]. For dalits, traditionally excluded from institutions controlling the village temple and tank, a place in the water users' association was a form of symbolic capital that mattered, perhaps more than the material gains from water. As an arena where subaltern aspirations for upward mobility and greater power within a Mudaliar-dominated village caste hierarchy could be pursued, the association's importance exceeded that of the resource it managed. Concerns about honour and respect, crystallised through a regionwide dalit movement, as much as the material practices of cultivation, became central to how water was managed. Cultural politics thus embeds resource struggles within a larger symbolic economy where the 'roles' that resources perform are several. Thus Iraq's invasion, while securing oil, also serves as an object lesson to impress the rest of the world with US willingness to act unilaterally—'defy us at your peril'. An 'environmental management programme' like the Madhya Pradesh Watershed Mission seeks to produce not only ecologically sustainable landscapes and livelihoods, but also legitimacy for the administration, distracting detractors from the state" s other practices that are ecologically and socially rapacious [Baviskar, *forthcoming* b]. At stake in resource politics are concerns that relate the materiality of the resource to wider structures of meaning. Following Bourdieu (1998), one must note that expanding die notion of value beyond the material does not mean that varied elements (honour, water, patronage, votes) can be assimilated into the same metric. On the contrary, it is precisely their difference and incommensurability that is fiercely guarded (e.g. honour loses its value and is compromised and corrupted if it is 'bought' or exchanged for money). Yet, political ecology often tends to analyses that distil meanings down to the economic 'last instance', rendering resources as sources of only profit and subsistence, and not social life. A cultural politics of natural resources treats identities, interests and resources, not as pre-detenniacd givens. But as emergent products of the practices of cultural production. By emphasising power, process and practice, this approach treats "culture itself as a site of political struggle" [Moore et al 2003:2]. The analytic draws attention to the cultural work involved in reproducing and challenging inequalities and exclusions around resources. It suggests that the practices of subject be understood not through structurally determined categories but through the specificity of their contradictory lived experience [Hak 1994]. While cultural politics shares political ecology's connitinent to understanding the asymmetric workings of power, it has a greater appreciation of the complex and contingent conditions under which people make history. Ethnography provides the tools best suited to represent that contingent process.

A Cultural Politics of Natural Resources

The analytic of cultural politics immediately draws attention to the presumptions contained in the term 'natural resources': 'natural' suggests an existence outside culture, something that is not an artefact of human making: an endowment of minerals, forest wealth or the bounty of rivers. 'Resources' invoke utility, culturally produced use and exchange values, something to be efficiently managed. Linking these antinomies are notions of property and possession, stewardship and responsibility, the right to use and appropriate. In turn, these notions rest upon assumptions about space and territory, and how they relate to collectivities in the past, present and future. These cultural formations have emerged over time and across spaces that are trans-local; they are always contentious and changing.

The following papers enable us to think anew the taken-for-granted aspects of natural resources. Originally written for a conference on 'Resources: Conceptions and Contestations', each essay can be read as an independent and self-contained argument. At the same time, each paper also highlights a different facet of the natural resources debate, a distinctive theme that may be summed up in a 'keyword'. Raymond Williams used this concept to explore 'significant, indicative words' whose changing meanings trace shifts in a vocabulary of cultural practices and institutions (1976: 15). The term 'natural resource' is a contemporary keyword which, when examined along with waste, scarcity, security, territory, sovereignty frontier, conflict, expertise and community, maps a distinctive world of meanings. Taken together, these related keywords chart out the terrain of the cultural politics of natural resources. In the following paragraphs, I outline the relations between these keywords, without attempting to summarise the papers.

The utilitarian principle of efficiency that dominates discourses around natural resources has an evil twin: waste. The necessity of avoiding waste entails the creation of subjects who understand that their role is to optimise the returns on a resource. As David Gilmartin argues through an account of British irrigation engineers in the Indus basin, differing conceptions of 'waste' were connected to competing visions of indigenous community. Waste was a term central to professional engineering theory as it developed in the 19th century. But it was a term critical also to the structure of the colonial state's revenue system, and to its reliance on the 'village community' as a key institution linking the state to the land. Controlling waste was, in differing ways, crucial to both an agenda of increasing 'scientific' control over the environment, and to the state's political manipulation of indigenous communities. Understanding the place of waste in colonial discourse is thus a way of understanding some of the most basic contradictions underlying this resource regime.

Like waste, scarcity is another keyword that defines a resource and shapes its disposition. Lyla Mehta points out that scarcity is not absolute nor 'natural'; its experience is always socially mediated. Tracing the cultural constructions of drought in Kutch, Mehta shows how changing modes of appropriating water have marginalised established practices of coping with the fluctuations in rainfall. Scarcity, earlier accepted as a fact of life and part of a frugal environment that affected everyone more or less equally, is now the focus of strenuous interventions that have exacerbated social differences. Intensive private water extraction has made scarcity 'real', a social fact that has consequences. The fortunes of the poorer households decline faster than the falling level of groundwater, and impoverished residents migrate outwards. At the same time, the spectre of scarcity is presented politically as a crisis, creating anxieties that demand dramatic resolution. Mehta argues that the construction of mega-dams like Sardar Sarovar is legitimised through such tactics that conceal the inequalities that have shaped scarcity in the first place.

The scarcity of natural resources has now begun to preoccupy another set of policy-makers besides conservationists and resource economists. In the post-cold war context, conflicts over natural resources are the focus of the geopolitics of security. Statements such as 'the next world war will be over water' assert a simplistic causal connection between resource scarcity and violence. Glossing over complex locally grounded cultural histories with which resource use is entangled, this alarmist rhetoric is usually accompanied by blueprints for action designed by the international development industry. So-called resource wars in 'weak states' like Sierra Leone are perceived as threatening international stability, necessitating authoritative interventions by the UN or the US. Simon Dalby shows how environmental security debates construct the problem in ways that obscure the links between 'zones of conflict' and global circuits of resource extraction and consumption.

The security debate presumes that a territory is discrete, and geography and communities can be isomorphically mapped onto each other. Natural resources are believed to 'belong' to localised political entities, a system of nation states and regions with clearly-defined proprietary powers to exclude others. Claims to territory are often based on the assertion of a 'sedentarist metaphysics' [Malkki 1992], primordial ties linking long-settled populations to landscapes. David Ludden offers a provocative challenge to this perspective by arguing that territoriality is, in fact, shaped by mobility. Delineating the long history of Sylhet, Bangladesh, he shows how the region is continually produced over time through far-flung webs of exchange. Commodity chains and circuits of labour move Sylheti resources around the world, contributing to the making of a distinctive place.

Integral to the notion of territory is that of sovereignty. Territory invokes a governable space within which populations and resources must be managed. And yet, as Michael Watts shows, the ordering processes suggested by Michel Foucault's concept of governmental rationality, a field of power aimed at shaping, guiding and directing conduct to achieve desired ends [Foucault 1991], collapse when multiple spatialities collide. Watts' discussion of oil politics in Nigeria examines governable spaces along three scales: chieftainship, indigeneity, and nationalism, marked by tensions and contradictions. In enclave economies where emerging ethnic identities challenge a rentier-state, violent youth gangs erupt like the gas flared from oil-rigs, illuminating Nigeria's great public secret—the fiction of the Nigerian nation.

The violence engendered around natural resources is most visible on the frontier, on the edge of wildness, where resources can be claimed by the resourceful and risk-taking. Frontiers are not given but are made—as the history of the American 'Wild West' shows, frontiers are constructed and conquered through violent acts of dispossession. Anna Tsing describes the making of a 'resource frontier' in Kalimantan, Indonesia, where Meratus Dayaks have experienced the takeover of their forests by armies, logging and plantation corporations, and mineral prospectors. Tsing provides a visceral account of the experience of the frontier, the instability and unevenness of its quicksilver changes. The myths of get-rich-quick is both intoxicating and terrifying; understanding it requires not only politics, but poetics. Resource frontiers are far away from the sanitised world of World Bank deliberations on 'natural resource management' and 'decentralised governance', and yet they are created in the spaces opened up when privatisation mixes with Indonesia's move from military dictatorship.

Conflict, generated as multiple groups lay claim—to natural resources, is at centre-stage in cultural politics. As much as the visible, violent confrontations between groups, cultural politics is concerned with the everyday ways in which conflict is negotiated, deflected or pre-empted. The absence of conflict may indicate not harmony, but 'symbolic violence' when relations of domination are transfigured into affective relations through socially-inculcated beliefs [Bourdieu 1998:102-103]. The different ways of dealing with conflict, from denial to warfare, form the substance of Michael Thompson's essay. Analysing climate change debates through the framework of Mary Douglas' cultural theory [Douglas and Wildavsky 1982], Thompson argues that disputes over the environment may not only be inevitable, but may also be desirable when argumentation leads to more constructive, democratic resolution. His paper makes a case for designing 'clumsy' institutions that accommodate the messy processes of airing and reconciling differences.

The process of decision-making around resource-related issues often accords great weight to expertise, privileging technocratic knowledge. 'Objective' scientific assessment is often legally mandated in the setting and monitoring of environmental standards. Scientific expertise shapes popular perceptions of 'problems'; its interventions organise experiences ranging from the human body (through medicine and public health) to the continental movement of rain and winds. The authority of science is summoned by governments, consumers, and environmentalists, often to opposing ends. Steve Rayner points out that in contemporary industrialised countries, as decision-makers have increasingly turned to scientific experts for resolving environmental issues, electoral participation has been decreasing. The rising reliance on expertise has been accompanied by declining accountability.

Rayner critically evaluates the ways in which governments have sought to incorporate public participation in the design of environmental decision-making.

Notions of participation presume a community of legitimate people who have rights. Cultural politics argues that the existence of such a community is not a foregone conclusion; the contentious processes of its being and becoming demand attention. Tania Li offers the tools to analyse how communities create legitimate identities in order to claim resources, and how conflicting images of community inspire different solidarities among environmentalists, human rights activists and government officials. Li presents a repertoire of terms—projects, practices, processes, positions—within a conceptualisation of power in terms of sovereignty, government and politics, enabling an empirical examination of particular resource struggles. Migrate farmers in Sulawesi, Indonesia, who occupy land inside a national park, land that is also claimed by an 'indigenous' group, have to muster a virtuous environmental persona in order to be recognised. Their calls for justice invoke citizenship, mimic indigeneity, and a history of displacement. From this creative pastiche of claims is community forged.

South Asia has been the locus of conceptually sophisticated and empirically rich research and social action about the politics of the environment. This collection of papers most based on research outside south Asia engages with the perspectives and issues that have been salient in this field. By emphasising the role of cultural politics, it attempts to take environmental debates onto grounds that may prove to be even more fertile.

2

Water Potentialities in India

Few undertakings offered a wider field for 'developing the resources of the country' in colonial India than the application of engineering science to large-scale irrigation works. No works were more spectacular than those that transformed the Punjab in the late 19th and early 20th century. In the 1880s, British engineers began the construction of a series of interlinked irrigation canals in western Punjab that eventually opened over 14 million acres of arid land to agricultural colonisation and settlement. The Punjab 'canal colonies', as these lands were called, emerged in colonial lore as one of the greatest success stories of colonial engineering, dramatising the productive potential of an alliance between the colonial state and scientific engineering in the development of India's resources. Here, truly, to transfer Donald Worster's phrase to a more appropriate context, were 'rivers of empire', harnessed by science and the imperial state to foster agricultural production.

But if the linking of science and empire conjures images of aggressive efforts to control and commodify nature in order to tap its productive powers, the history of the Punjab canal colonies in fact suggests the complex character of the relationship between the state, science and nature in the colonial context. On one level, colonial water engineering in the Punjab grew out of emerging 19th century European ideas about the relationship between science and political economy more broadly. These ideas defined Punjab's river waters as a 'resource', open to increasing state control for purposes of productive 'use' and 'development'. But if, as James Thomason noted, 'developing' such resources was critical to enhanced income, it was also critical to new forms of state power. Increasing state control over water—and thus over the land—defined new frameworks for the exercise of control over the local 'communities' comprising Indus basin society. The role of resource control in the simultaneous agendas of enhancing productivity and of increasing state control was in fact one that was marked by serious contradictions. While the application of engineering science allowed the state to commodify water in new ways, it also impinged on the structures through which the state had long sought to define its political relationship to indigenous society, and to the kin-based village 'communities' that comprised it. The contradictory character of colonial thinking about nature—and, by implication, the contradictory meanings attached by the colonial state to notions of 'development'—is the focus of this paper. It is the argument of this paper that these contradictions can be highlighted by focusing on the foundational usage in the colonial context of one key term—the word 'waste'. This was a term central to professional engineering theory as it developed in the 19th century. But it was a term critical also to the structure of the colonial state's revenue system, and to its reliance on the 'village community' as a central institution linking the state to the land. Controlling 'waste' was, in differing ways, central to both an agenda of increasing 'scientific' control over the environment, and to the state's political manipulation of indigenous communities. Understanding the place of 'waste' in colonial discourse is thus a key to the understanding of some of the most basic contradictions underlying the colonial resource regime.

Science and Irrigation Engineering

North-west India was one of the great experimental centres for irrigation engineering in the late 19th century—and one in which science and professional engineering played a major role. Irrigation investment in India was hardly new in the mid-19th century; the East India Company had been involved in a number of irrigation projects, largely planned and executed by military engineers, many trained at the East India Company's military college at Addiscombe. The emergence of a professional cadre of civil irrigation engineers in India can perhaps best be dated from the opening in 1848 of the College of Civil Engineering at Roorkee (renamed the Thomason College of Civil Engineering in 1854). The founding of the college was directly linked to the growing demand for irrigation engineers created by the construction of the Ganges canal in the 1840s, but it was reorganised and expanded in the 1850s with the irrigation requirements of the newly-annexed Punjab, and its newly established public works department, also in mind.

Not all new PWD engineers came from Roorkee, particularly after the founding in 1871 of a new engineering college at Cooper's Hill in England funded by the Government of India. But as the histories of both Roorkee and Cooper's Hill demonstrated, colonialism in India encouraged the professionalisation of British civil engineering generally, and suggested the profession's important colonial roots. As Richard Temple noted, Britain had held, as late as the 1880s, a reputation for backwardness in technical education compared with the countries of continental Europe, since most engineering instruction tended to be conducted in 'private establishments at the industrial centres of England', and was geared largely towards private employment. But in India, the British government had come to have, as Temple wrote in 1883, 'colossal interests at stake in its public works', with a concomitant need for well-educated engineers and 'immense resources for so arranging its plans that this object shall be secured'. From the beginning this promised to give to engineers trained at Roorkee and Cooper's Hill a new sense of professional mission, and one intimately linked to colonialism.

Mathematics, the language of international science, lay at the heart of this education. Many Roorkee professors, who tended to come initially from the Royal Engineers, held, in the words of William Willcocks, an early Roorkee graduate, aspirations for 'world-wide science'. Doubtless, military irrigation engineers in India had long had an interest in what could be learned pragmatically from irrigation works in other parts of the world, but in the last decades of the 19th century this was linked to a growing sense of shared expertise drawn from a common body of 'theoretical' (that is, mathematical) published research. As Willcocks wrote of his days as a student at Roorkee in the early 1870s, "we were taught on the sound lines of the Ecole Polytechnique in Paris, and not on the ridiculous lines generally in vogue in England at the time".

On one level, of course, the increasing prestige and professionalism of irrigation engineers in India in the late 19th century was rooted particularly in the conjoining of the prestige of mathematical science to the prestige of service to the state. Central to this was a, 'public' commitment to scientific control over nature, a commitment linked to service to the state, which worked powerfully on British and Indians alike. It was the ethos of disinterested service to science that empowered the self-image of many engineers as engaged in a moral enterprise, "content", as one engineer put it, "to let their achievements speak for themselves" even as they identified strongly with the power of the state. For many Indians, like Ram Das Tandon, who graduated from Roorkee in 1898 and joined the Punjab Irrigation Department, the process of becoming an engineer at the college was like passing through a transformative 'dream', defining an entirely new 'public' identity. For British boys at Cooper's Hill, as Temple wrote, the aim of education was not just skill in engineering, but also the 'moral training' and 'discipline' that would prepare them for 'victorious success'—success, in this case, in 'subduing' nature,.and turning its products into 'resources' that could be used for purposes of production. But it was a commitment to mathematical science that most clearly defined their distinctive professional image. As a Punjab Irrigation Department manual later suggested in tracing the development of irrigation engineering in the Punjab, the military engineers who had worked in the mid-19th century had shown 'amazing courage and resources', but 'their knowledge of irrigation and hydraulics was nil'. They worked largely by trial and error. The Bari Doab and Sirhind canals had thus been built with 'beautifully drawn and skilfully coloured plans', but with 'shocking mistakes of design', which had been corrected only by trial and error and dogged persistence. It was only mathematical science that had moved engineering beyond this phase, so that it could be said by the 1880s that irrigation engineering as a profession was really 'on its feet'.

Water's Duty: Language of Engineering Control

The vision of man's relationship to nature that underlay the professionalisation of irrigation engineering in the second half of the 19th century was perhaps clearest in the metaphorical language that came to define the foundations of irrigation science. Perhaps no single term was more redolent of the underlying assumptions that shaped water engineering in the late 19th century than the term 'duty', a word that assumed foundational significance in the 19th century development of mathematical irrigation science. While the term echoed the sense of moral mission increasingly important in the public profession of science, the word 'duty' was defined in technical jargon as applying directly to water; it was, in fact, the basic measure of water as a 'resource', that is, the measure of the productive 'use' to which irrigation water was put. Water 'duty' was, in the words of one leading engineer, the measure of "the relation between the volume of water and the area of crop which it matures". Though its precise measurement varied somewhat in different contexts, it was usually expressed in India in terms of the number of acres of cropped land that a cusec of water could be expected to bring to maturity in a particular period of time: thus, "if 1 cubic foot a second [cusec] running continuously for four months will mature 100 acres of crop, the 'duty', in that case, is said to be 100 acres to the cusec, to the base of 4 months". 'Duty' was thus a fundamental measure of the ultimate goal of irrigation science—the extraction of productive capacity from nature. As Herbert Wilson noted in a leading irrigation engineering textbook of the late 19th century, "On the duty of water depends the financial success of every irrigation enterprise, for as water becomes scarce its value increased. In order to estimate the cost of irrigation in projecting works, it is essential to know how much water the land will require. In order to ascertain the dimensions of canals and reservoirs for the irrigation of given areas the duty of water must be known".

The prominent use of the term 'duty' in water engineering suggested the discipline's close connections to trends that had transformed 19th century scientific conceptions of nature more generally. Most critically, it suggested the vital importance of measurement as scientific engineering's defining feature. But it also suggested the metaphoric vision of natural systems that increasingly influenced the world-view of 19th century engineers. In origin, the term 'duty' was one that was first technically applied in Britain in the late 18th century as a measurement for assessing the efficiency of steam engines. As used by James Watt, for example, the efficiency of a steam engine in pumping water was measured by the 'duty' (or work) it could perform: the number of pounds of water that the engine could raise one foot per bushel of coal as fuel. The concept of 'duty' was thus rooted in the concern for the efficiency of energy use within a closed mechanical system.

The foundational usage of 'duty' in late 19th century irrigation engineering transformed its meaning in critical ways. But its use in irrigation engineering nevertheless suggested the firm grounding of the discipline in the larger transformations in British scientific thinking about energy that marked the middle decades of the 19th century and that shaped the broader professionalisation of engineering. As M. Norton Wise and Crosbie Smith have argued, these decades witnessed a fundamental shift in the dominant view of nature among scientists from one stressing a mechanical 'balance' of natural forces, tending toward equilibria (a vision dating back to Newton's clockwork universe), to one that stressed the importance in nature of perpetual change and of the tendency of natural systems to move relentlessly toward energy dissipation. In the realm of scientific thinking, this shift was captured perhaps most prominently in the articulation at mid-century of the second law of thermodynamics—which postulated, through the concept of entropy, the fundamental notion of natural energy systems tending towards ever-increasing disorder. The science of energy conservation and control thus came to be central to scientific technique in the 19th century; 'work' and 'waste', as Wise and Smith argue, emerged as the critical terms defining human interactions with nature, even as these came to be increasingly central also in shaping thinking about the human economies through which production was organised. As a result, the early to mid-19th century tended to witness a gradual shift from the clock (which mechanically suggested nature's 'balance') to the engine (whose purpose was production) as a root metaphor for conceptualising human relations with nature in mechanical terms. And with this, the extraction of 'work' for human use and the minimisation of 'waste' from the energies of nature came to define the mission of the professional engineer.

With its emphasis on water's 'duty' as the fundamental measure of irrigational value, irrigation engineering clearly imported this engine model into its own metaphorical language. Canal systems, like machines, drew on nature's energy, in this case the productive, life-giving power of scarce water, carried through river systems. The central technique of water engineering was thus geared toward building structures, and mathematically modelling water flow, so as to maximise the productive work that water could perform. "We may look on (a canal system) as a great machine composed of many parts", wrote one prominent engineer in the 1870s, "and go about calculating its efficiency much in the same way as that of a steam-engine". The moral imperative of irrigation engineering was to counter the natural tendency of water, like energy, to run to waste. As Bruno Latour has put it, any good water engineer "should begin with the principle that if water can leak away, it will". It was this preoccupation—with thwarting the natural tendency towards waste—that defined both the moral mission of most irrigation engineers and their discipline as a mathematical craft (a craft concerned with using mathematics first to model nature to understand its processes, and then to construct mechanical means to tap its energy, as a resource for productive use).

Such a vision of 'waste'—and a concern for making efficient use of scarce resources—held implications also for how users themselves were incorporated into such a system. Fundamental to the notion of duty was that efficiency depended not just on the flow of water in canals and distributaries, but also on how water was used in farmers' fields. As a mathematical construct, the 'duty' of water depended critically on efficiency of individual use, for it was only when water reached the root zones of plants in individual fields that its productive energies were unleashed. As Herbert Wilson noted in a late 19th century irrigation textbook, calculations of 'duty' thus depended not just on the soil, the rainfall, and the condition of the ditches, but also on 'the skill of the irrigator'. Measurements of duty inevitably hinged on calculations of 'waste' (water losses) in all the parts of canal systems, including the irrigators' fields. R.G. Kennedy, later chief engineer of the Punjab, estimated in 1883 that for every 100 cubic feet of water entering the Bari Doab canal at its river intake at Madhopur, 20 cubic feet were lost in transit in the main canal, 6 cubic feet in 'rajbahas' (distributaries), 21 cubic feet in village watercourses, and 25 cubic feet by waste in everyday usage, thus yielding an overall efficiency rating for 'the canal as a machine' (or duty measured at the canal intake) of 28 percent. Duty could only be measured when all these variables (and others) were taken into account.

But the place of the user in such calculations—however important in theory—remained in practice highly problematic. Textbook engineering doctrine in the late 19th century hinged on a vision of the user as a maximising producer, who was thus joined with the engineer (in theory) in a community defined by a common struggle for production against a wasteful nature. The language of opposition between engineering science and natural 'waste' paralleled the dominant language of market efficiency shaping late 19th century ideas of political economy and economic man. But in practice, colonial engineers rarely incorporated users effectively into their formulas for canal design, or, in fact, into their thinking about the efficient control of water as a resource.

On one level, this was the result of the virtually insurmountable practical problems that engineers faced in delivering water in measurable quantities to individual users. Only by providing a measured volume of water to each user could canal administrators charge for water in such a way as to create incentives for individual producers to behave as profit maximisers, thus maximising the efficiency of use and distribution within larger irrigation systems. But in practice, colonial irrigation engineers despaired in the first half of the 20th century of devising a practical system of water gauging that was both tamper-proof, and inexpensive enough to be used effectively for measuring the quantities of water delivered to individuals. Though they repeatedly remarked on the inefficiencies in water use encouraged by the absence of volumetric water charges in the Indus basin (and proposed numerous hypothetical expedients for gauging water so that users would be forced to pay for the actual quantities of water consumed), they never developed the mechanical or social technology to solve this problem. Water charges in the Indus basin were thus in practice taken, throughout the colonial period and beyond, not on quantities of water used, but on the basis of matured crop areas under irrigation. This had the advantage of linking water charges to the actual 'work' that water performed (in terms of crop returns), but it undercut all efforts to encourage (or measure) individual human efficiency as a vital part of the overall irrigating 'machine'. Indeed, to the extent that engineers were able to encourage non-wasteful water use in individual fields, it was not by incorporating irrigators into the larger structure of the 'machine', but rather by laying down bureaucratic (and often unenforceable) rules for non-wasteful water application.

Failure to incorporate individuals effectively into the 'irrigating machine' in fact led to the assignment of a prominent place in irrigation structures to the 'community' of irrigators occupying the lands lying beyond departmentally controlled canal outlets. Given the technical constraints within which they operated, most engineers in fact came to view their responsibility for maintaining the irrigating 'machine' as ending, basically, at the canal outlet. This did not mean that engineers were totally unconcerned with the distribution and use of water beyond the outlet. To oversee distribution, engineers often designed *'warabandis'*, or schedules of turns for water, which were intended to regulate the quantities of water (or, more accurately, the times of access to water) which were available to each field, and thus to each individual, on the watercourses attached to each canal outlet. But in practice such schedules were rarely rigidly enforced (nor carefully monitored). Indeed, official engineering law and practice empowered British officials to frame such warabandis "only when communities of irrigators themselves specifically asked for help in preparing them. Whatever the contours of engineering theory, in practice engineers thus delivered water not so much to individuals (though it was individual 'occupiers' who paid water charges), but rather to measured quantities of land (or 'chaks'), which were attached to each outlet, and assigned water on the basis of calculations of duty and irrigation intensity. From this perspective, the success of irrigation was measured less by its role in delivering water to individuals to be put to maximum productive 'use', and more in terms of the total quantities of unproductive land—'wasteland'—that were brought under irrigation. Engineers thus commonly measured irrigation works by the gross areas of land brought under irrigation 'command', even as the local control and distribution of water was to an important degree left to the collective organisation of communities of users.

Opening the maximum quantity of 'wasteland' to cultivation possible—and thus bringing this land within the structure of British revenue administration—had long been an overriding concern of the Indus basin administration. In using this as a measure of the success of irrigation works, engineers were in some ways simply adapting to the political and social circumstances in which they operated. As one engineer puts it, engineers had long recognised the importance of practical adaptation to the success of their craft; professional engineering was, after all, in the end nothing but 'a blending of theory and practice'.

But the role of the individual producer and the local 'community' in Indus basin irrigation nevertheless remained a focus of considerable uncertainty and unease among Indus basin engineers. However important the role that the local community came to play in organising the use of water beyond the outlet, the idea of community control at this level had no formal, theoretical purchase within the technical metaphor of the irrigating 'machine'. In practice, the local community stood as a hinge at the heart of the system, facilitating on one level the actual delivery of water to the fields, but disrupting, on another level, the community of production—defined by a common commitment to the control of nature's waste—that linked the engineer and the maximising individual producer in engineering theory.

The implications of this for the overall workings of Punjab's irrigation systems were substantial. But the significance of this lay not just in the practical difficulties in realising the structure of engineering, but in the interface that this defined between the structure of irrigation theory and the structure of colonial political administration. Communities were, of course, in practice, highly varied. But if the local community had no formal place in engineering theory, it had long occupied a critical place in the structure of colonial thinking about political control in the Indus basin. In administrative terms, the irrigation chak to which engineers delivered water in the canal colonies was largely synonymous with the 'mauza', or village estate, which held a central place in the politics of colonial revenue collection and administration. To analyse the impact of the community on irrigation, we thus need to analyse the important place that this vision of local community held within the structure of colonial administration, and how this, too, related to a vital set of colonial ideas about production, nature and the land. To analyse the development of colonial political theory too broadly would take us well beyond the scope of this article. But to look at the local community as a central element in the structure of British rule—and how it related to a different set of ideas about nature and production from those fostered by the theory of professional engineering—we can do no better than to look once again, in a different context this time, at a single, critically important word: the term 'waste'.

Village 'Waste' and Village Producer

To understand the distinctive meaning of 'waste' in the British revenue system one must begin with the primacy in British revenue administration given to the village. The 'village' and the 'village community' defined the bedrock of the colonial social and property order. Individual agricultural producers and property holders were critical to the British property system, but they were almost invariably conceptualised by the British as being embedded in villages, and villages were defined in British eyes by the existence of village communities.

Defining the meaning of 'village community', however, is hardly a straightforward enterprise, nor was it so for the British in the mid-19th century. When the British first began to survey the land of the Punjab in the middle decades of the 19th century, they had found an immense variety of structures of social relationships and adaptations to the land. The presence of extensive forms of cultivation, linked to semi-pastoralism, was particularly important in many parts of Punjab. If 'villages' had an essential feature, it was that each village engendered, in the very particularism of its relationship to its physical and social environment, identities that were discrete from those of all other villages.

But the British nevertheless sought in the village a local frame that would serve the purposes of what James Scott has called, 'state simplification'. Partly, the British achieved this through theoretical speculation about the evolutionary relationships that defined unifying patterns of variation in local social organisation, patterns shaped both by relationships to nature and to previous states. This found a prominent place in many late 19th century settlement reports, and laid the groundwork for much anthropological speculation about the general character of variation in local communities. But more important than this, the British themselves gave to villages a common form that essentialised the category in the administration of colonial Punjab—a form defined by maps. Whatever their variations, the one thing that all villages came to have in common under the British was that they were territorially bounded and mapped; the term 'village' in fact became synonymous administratively with a mapped territory (known technically as a mauza, or village estate). This created the framework within which the term 'village community' came to have legal meaning within the colonial system, and it played an important role also ultimately in shaping the meaning of irrigation chaks.

The mauza, or village estate, became the local arena within which individual private property was defined, mapped and recorded, this was the realm in which individual producers resided. In this sense, it was an administrative frame that had no necessary connection to local community at all. Though the British sometimes made use of collective village responsibility in the collection of the revenue, the mapped village estate created a framework within which judiciable rights to individual property were virtually always clearly and separately recorded. Each mauza's property owners were bound directly and individually to the state—both by a common interest in the enforcement of individual property law, and by a common commitment to the productive land use necessary for the payment of revenue. A nexus of law and agricultural productivity binding the individual property holder and the state together was in fact central to the 'public' identity of the state itself, and to the definition of the individual owner as producer. It was in this sense that the law created a framework for the definition of the productive, maximising individual who was theoretically critical to engineering theory.

And yet at the same time the recognition of the village as a vessel for local 'community' was also central to the British framework of administration. Recognition of the bonds of local community was vital to the political structure of the state, for this created the framework within which the British established structures of local leadership and 'representation'. But critical also to the structure of colonial rule was the grounding of local community in a conceptual arena that would not encroach on the contractual relations linking the individual and the state within the colonial revenue system. 'Community', as the British saw it, was thus grounded in a metaphorical field entirely separate from the realm of production—in the field of 'blood' and genealogy.

Critically for the structure of colonial power, this realm too was knowable by the British through careful administrative research and 'objective' framing. Just as the land of villages was mapped, the 'blood' of the village proprietors was also mapped through the recording of genealogies, which became a vital part of every settlement record. Genealogies were in fact often used to trace the village proprietors to a single ancestor or group of ancestors who had originally occupied the land and founded the village. "Village by village", Clive Dewey writes, "the Settlement Officers and their assistants traced the descent of rights and the descent of right-holders back to some mythical founder...". Such stories of the original breaking up and settling of the land were central to the grounding of communities on the land. But the essence of community for the British generally lay not in the process of attachment to the land, but rather in the recorded genealogical tables themselves. "A glance at them will tell the history of a village", wrote one settlement officer. If history is a charter for community, then this was a very distinctive notion of 'history'. But it was one that supported the distinctive vision of 'village community' that the British were in process of shaping. While bonds of law and productivity bound the state and the individual, the legal existence of the community came to lie in a separate conceptual space—in the bonds of kinship.

The conceptual separation of local community from the realm of production was sustained by the colonial development of a dual system of property law. While individual rights of landed property were rooted in the law of contracts (and were based on state recognition of individual property rights in return for the regular payment of revenue), relations of community were regulated through a system of 'customary law', whose underlying principles were driven, as British legal theorists argued, by the dynamics of kinship. At the heart of customary law were a series of presumptions about the conveyance of property (primarily through inheritance) that were aimed towards the maintenance of patrilineal authority in the village, largely through the denial of virtually all landholding rights to women. While the British thus conceptualised the original establishment of property rights as rooted in a contract between the state and the landowner as a rational producer, they conceptualised customary inheritance law as rooted in the organic bonds of 'primitive' community. In his capacity as a member of the village community, the landowner was thus not a rational maximiser; to the contrary, he was a patriarch who acted only according to the logic of 'blood'.

The complexity in this historic separation of genealogical community from the realm of production is suggested by the recent work of Richard Saumarez Smith, who has closely analysed one of the earliest British settlements in the Punjab. Smith has suggested that in many villages, issues of productivity and community were, at the time of the British arrival, often closely linked. In villages in Ludhiana, Smith found that 'shares' in village assets were calculated originally in terms of 'ploughs', thus reflecting a system organised by "the business of agricultural production, with shares based on the productive capabilities of individual members". But British policy tended to shift the language of local community and of 'shares' in village assets from one based on productive participation in the village, to one based on recorded genealogy and descent. As they recorded them at settlement, the British used the definition of ancestral shares in the village largely to mark out a distinct community of village proprietors, that is, 'owners' (as distinct from 'tenants', who now had no shares in the village, whatever their actual contributions to the process of production). Shares thus carried increasingly small significance in terms of a community of village production; they were, rather, attached to individual proprietary holdings that were mapped on the land and heritable in perpetuity. In order to map out clear individual rights to property, in other words, for purposes of establishing contractual revenue obligations, the British shifted the language of 'community' into an arena, 'blood', that was, at least in law and theory, entirely separable from the process of production.

But what, then, in British eyes, was the stake of the genealogically-based 'community' in the land and assets of the village? This is where the concept of 'waste' came to play a critical and central role in British thinking. As the British mapped the villages of the Punjab, they delineated distinctive categories of land that reflected the oppositions between individual, private property and the genealogically-based 'village community' that marked the British property system more generally in the second half of the 19th century. Critical to this was the demarcation of what was known as the village 'commons', the *'shamilat deh'*, a category of land widely referred to by the British as the village 'waste'.

In the mapping of villages, the delineation of individual property, and the delineation of the 'village waste' were in fact inseparably linked. The first aim of British settlement officers when they mapped Punjabi villages was to sort out the claims of villagers to land held in individual 'proprietary right'. This was, by definition, land that was potentially productive and assessable to British revenue (subject, in other words, to individual contract). The 'commons', as a legal category, basically represented that land which was left over. It was thus, by definition, 'wasteland', that is, land on which claims to productive use (and thus to individual proprietorship) could not be, or had not been, effectively made.

As a village institution, the extent of the 'commons' also depended on the external demarcation of the mauza (and thus depended also on the definition by the British of the village as a mapped structure). In areas of the Punjab where uncultivated land was plentiful (which included large parts of the province at the middle of the 19th century), the regular British practice was to assign significant blocks of this 'waste' to village estates according to general formula. "Where the waste was of small extent", Baden-Powell wrote, "the whole of the adjoining area was included in the village-boundary as a matter of course; where it was extensive, each village received twice, and, in some cases, thrice, the cultivated area". But whether defined in relationship to proprietary holdings, or to the external boundary of the village, the official marking out of the shamilat as commons, or joint share-held property, had far more to do with the legal distinction between production and waste, than with a history of actual common use.

'Commons' and 'wasteland' thus tended to become legally synonymous on village land in the Punjab. This, of course, did not mean that 'waste' held the same meanings for all. For the British, the association of the term 'waste' with common land was one with long historical antecedents in England itself. But in 19th century Punjab, the term 'waste' subsumed a number of indigenous terms, for the indigenous cultural meanings attached to the oppositions between cultivated and uncultivated land were complex. Uncultivated land in Punjab varied from *'banjar jadid'*, or 'short fallows', that might have been cultivated relatively recently, to *'jangal'*, which signified barren scrub land, not subject to cultivated control (in revenue parlance, *'ghair mumkin'*, 'without possibility' of cultivation, which also included roads, the village site or sites, etc). Though in much of western and southern Punjab, large chunks of shamilat were carved from bar jangal, in much of central Punjab village shamilat was constituted primarily from land referred to as *'banjar qadim'*, or 'long fallows'. The term 'long fallows' suggested an opposition between village shamilat and cultivated, proprietary land, that was far less sharp than that suggested by the term 'wasteland'. Such land was often vitally important to village production, used not only for grazing of plough and well animals, but also, in some cases, readily transformable to banjar jadid under pressure of increasing family sizes or in the event of greater availability of water. But all this nevertheless tended to be subsumed under the larger English rubric, 'waste'.

Most British officials knew full well that 'wasteland' was not always without important uses; it was they, after all, who in their revenue records often explicated the nuances of indigenous terminology for 'wasteland'. But the logic of the binary distinction between proprietary land and 'wasteland' was in fact one that gained powerful saliency from the internal logic of the colonial property system. By classifying land as 'waste', the British marked it, in effect, as outside the realm of production and therefore, by definition, outside the realm also of individual property. And in so doing, they made the land available as an arena for the definition of a different kind of property—'community' property. Village 'commons' thus became the ground on which the existence of a 'village community' was inscribed. Through the delineation of the 'commons', the shares of the proprietors in the village community as a whole were marked symbolically on the map of the village estate, and by classifying the commons as 'waste' the British made clear that the realm of community was in fact quite distinct from the realm of production. The labelling of the commons as 'waste', as a product of nature without productive use. In fact made possible the definition of the village 'community' itself as an organic, 'primitive', kinship-based construction, defining the 'communal' man, in effect, as the antithesis of the rational producer.

In actual practice, of course, the role of the village commons and the village community in production was complex and highly variable, as Minoti Chakravarty-Kaul has demonstrated. In arid western Punjab (and in parts of southern and eastern Punjab as well), the use of common land was often intimately connected to the interactions between pastoralism and agriculture. In some Punjab villages, the management of the commons was critical to the maintenance of individual household production and was closely integrated into community management of other productive resources. Private plots were often scattered in eastern and central Punjabi villages to equalise access to varying qualities of land, including the village commons. 'Collective management' of the commons, which was normally kept in relatively compact blocks, often went hand in hand in such villages with the collective village management of other productive resources, such as 'field channels of irrigation wells and ponds'. Income from common lands, whether from grazing fees from outsiders or from rents charged to 'kamins' i.e. village servants), supported collective village management expenses. To suggest that British attempts to legally situate the shamilat on the 'waste' defined a form of 'commons' that had oo rebbonship to production, would seriously distort the realities of village life.

But the British were, in general, both interested in the administration of this collective realm, which was quite ancillary to their emerging vision of the village—Many officials undoubtedly recognised that the commons was in some instances an important productive adjunct to agriculture organisation (particularly for agriculture depending on animal-powered wells), and 'rights' of access to the canal were often recorded in the *'wajib-ul-arz'* (the village 'record of rights'). These also became at times an issue of some importance in litigation in the British courts. But the structure of law, as officials themselves noted, offered little to support the coilectne management of the commons. That the commons woefaraurc important to the British as a symbolic field for the imi ilpion of community defined by ancestral shares was suggested by the fact that in many villages, areas of 'waste' were defined as 'commons' not only for the village as a whole, but for the Many constitutive genealogical segments of villages (called 'pattis' or 'tarafs'), as well. Customary law, which was constructed largely in the language of 'rights', offered few legal remedies whereby the village community as a whole could take productive control of the commons and administer it for joint benefit. With increasing pressure to bring the commons into the realm of production, almost the only legal remedy that British law had to offer was partition of the commons into individual proprietary holdings. And ironically, while often precipitated by bitter conflict among the proprietors of the village (or between themselves and their tenants or 'kamins'), partition by shares offered at least a symbolic reaffirmation of the idea that the ancestral proprietors in fact continued to embody the village community as a whole. While forms of collective village action and organisation were thus common enough in the Punjab, the legal definition of local community had moved in another direction. The effect of British colonial policy in the Punjab was to shift the legal meaning of village community out of the arena of production, and into a realm of genealogy that was largely divorced from questions of production and management. Within this framework, community was defined, at least in theory, in relation to a conception of nature far different from that which defined the alliance of engineer and individual in emerging engineering theory. Community was inscribed on the land only where the individualism of man's productive relations to nature was kept at bay (on the 'waste'), not through the act of conquering and subduing nature's inherent 'wasteful' tendencies. Whatever the attitudes of local villagers towards nature (and these were no doubt various), the structure of British power had itself defined large structures of integration that incorporated and organised community in sharply contradictory ways.

Conclusion

Contrasting colonial usages of the term 'waste' thus suggests, in the end, contradictions that were inherent in state efforts to incorporate local community organisation into the structure of Punjab's newly engineered irrigation systems. In systems designed to control nature's 'waste', engineers sought to deliver water to maximising individual water users and property controllers. Indeed, at the heart of engineering doctrine, as a historical development, was the notion of a moral community of engineers and producers, linked together by their perception of nature as a field whose 'waste' needed to be contained in the interests of promoting human happiness. In theory, Punjabi farmers were potentially as much a part of such a community as European producers; the very definition of property in the colonial system was in part predicated on the vision of the individual as a maximising producer.

Yet, in spite of this, local 'communities', had in practice come to play central and disruptive roles in these systems. Recognising the difficulty of delivering measured quantities of water to individual users, engineering doctrine came to emphasise the importance of delivering water to outlets, beyond which lay 'communities' of water users. Some engineers conceptualised these local communities as part of the larger community of interests linking producers and engineers; indeed, some engineers saw the drawing up of 'warabandis' as a step towards defining local communities of interest in production that were rooted in the common drive to minimise waste. And yet, the effort to incorporate such local communities into a state system of irrigation management ran up against another definition of community that was already firmly entrenched on the ground and linked to the political structure of colonial property. This was the village community, a structure defined by a very different definition of the term, 'waste'. Within the property order of the British state, the local community was defined not in relation to a system of local production, but rather in relationship to genealogy—and it was associated pre-eminently not with productive village land, but with common land labelled as 'waste'. Whatever the actual roles of village institutions in matters of production, the 'village community' as a legal entity was conceptualised by the state as fundamentally non-productive and rooted in an entirely different conception of nature from that defining the mathematics of engineering. And given this structure, it is little wonder—whatever the important practical difficulties engineers faced with the pricing and delivery of water to individual villagers—that most engineers avoided interference in village affairs. Efforts to incorporate local communities into the structure of irrigation thus proved problematic at best.

To detail the administrative problems engineers have encountered in the 20th century in incorporating local communities into the massive, integrated irrigation systems of the Indus basin would take us well beyond the scope of this article. Suffice it to say that these have been considerable. Whatever the state's role in bringing large new areas under irrigation, and in increasing aggregate agricultural production, its inability to use engineering science to break through the power of local village communities and extend a technical system of irrigation control into the villages has sometimes been seen as a failure of development. But it would be a mistake to see these processes as defined by the tension between development on the one hand, and indigenous community on the other. In assessing the colonial system, we must ask whether the contradictions that have led to these problems were not intrinsic to the very conception of development. The colonial property system laid the foundations for the extension of an engineering vision into the villages by defining a structure of landed property that was predicated on the existence of rational, economic producers. This was at the heart of effective state power and revenue collection, and it was also central to the process, as James Thomason put it in the quotation opening this article, of 'developing the resources of the country'. But the very logic of this process demanded that the state relegate, for its own political purposes, the legal meaning of community to a very different realm, the primitive and non-productive realm of genealogy and 'blood'. Reflecting the imperatives of colonial rule, this too was a product of development.

3

Multi-faceted Nature of Water Scarcity

Introduction

Water scarcity is considered one of the most pressing problems confronting the survival of humankind in the next century. But what is it that makes water scarce? It is the rapidly dwindling aquifers? Is it the billion-plus people who lack access to clean water? Clearly, water supplies are limited and finite, but does this make water scarce in absolute terms? By focusing on the case of 'water-scarce' Kutch in India and its relationship with the controversial Sardar Sarovar Project (SSP), the paper argues that access to and control over water is usually linked to prevailing social and power relations which influence how it is used or abused. The paper demonstrates that water scarcity can be constructed differently by different social and political actors, often to meet political ends. Through a detailed empirical and multi-sited examination of both actual practices and discourses around scarcity in the Kutch region of western India, the paper argues that scarcity is both 'real' and 'constructed'. The paper analyses the 'real' aspects of scarcity—dwindling groundwater aquifers, increased salinity—while also revealing the means by which scarcity is 'constructed' or 'manufactured' through political and policy processes. State discourses portray scarcity as natural (rather than human-induced) and chronic (rather than cyclical). The external 'essentialised' notions of scarcity generated by state discourse and state programmes are often quite different from local people's knowledge systems and livelihood strategies that allow them to adapt to the unpredictability and temporary scarcity of water. This paper begins by discussing the multifaceted nature of scarcity and then provides an overview of Kutch, its water resources and the links with the SSP. It then analyses the dominant discourses of scarcity and demonstrates what they obscure. The paper then examines local responses to scarcity and ends with a discussion of how socio-political, discursive and institutional factors have successfully combined to naturalise scarcity in Kutch.

Multi-faceted Nature of Scarcity

From once being considered an abundant resource, water is increasingly seen as a 'scarce' resource, which needs to be managed judiciously. The statistics are well known: only 3 per cent of water on earth is fresh and most of this is locked away in the ice caps of Antarctica and Greenland or deep in underground aquifers. As a result only 0.3 per cent of global water is available for human consumption [Gleick 1993:3]. Water scarcity, as it is constructed in global declarations and debates, is often presented in absolute and monolithic terms, obscuring the complex nature of scarcity and its linkages with ecological, socio-political, temporal and anthropogenic dimensions. Let us review some of them.

One, unlike other environmental resources such as forests and coal, water is a renewable resource, which means that its availability is constantly subjected to variation depending on its state in the hydrological cycle. (One exception is groundwater, which is less renewable than other water sources.) Not only is its state variable (e.g., solid, fluid, or in gas form) but it is also variable across time and space, depending on factors such as climate, season and temperature. These are the biophysical and ecological attributes determining water availability.

Two, water scarcity has temporal and cyclical dimensions. People living in arid and semi-arid regions have long since recognised the temporal nature of water scarcity as the case study demonstrates. Periods of dearth are interspersed by periods of abundance. Water availability, thus, is characterised by uncertainty in many parts of the world. However, while the contingency on factors such as rainfall, vegetation and grass cover make water availability uncertain, it would be fallacious to see water scarcity as something that is constant and permanent. This is because supplies do become abundant in favourable seasons and climatic conditions. Thus, water supplies are relative to exogenous factors such as rainfall.

The third dimension is the distributional and relational aspects of scarcity. There is tremendous inequality in access to and control over water resources. Scarcity is not felt universally by all. In water scarce western India, irrigation pumps work twenty-four hours a day, while poor women find their drinking wells run dry. In arid parts of the world, people consume 10 litres of water per day [Mehta forthcoming] while an average American, by contrast, uses over 700 litres a day [Gleick 1993:375].

The fourth dimension concerns the anthropogenic dimensions of scarcity. While water scarcity tends to be naturalised today, its anthropogenic dimensions are whitewashed. It is well known that the degradation of the Aral Sea and the Caspian Sea are largely due to human intervention. Furthermore, many of the silted up dams, broken hand-pumps and defunct water pipeline schemes are indicative of bad management practices and/or a failure to encourage or create supportive institutional arrangements to govern water supplies. In sum, it is wrong to conceive of water scarcity in absolute terms, but instead there is an urgent need to link water scarcity with socio-political, institutional and hydrological factors.

Water Scarcity as Socially and Politically Constructed

Scarcity is frequently considered a 'given' factor of human life and an existential reality. It is also one of the main premises of modern economic thought. Even some sociologists have been seduced by these ideas and see the combat against scarcity to be the basis of social action [cf Balla 1981:225]. However, has it always been so? Nicholas Xenos in the work Scarcity and Modernity (1989) systematically shows how certain attributes of modernity have given rise to the universal notion of scarcity. Today unshaken belief in paradigms promoted by neo-classical economics makes scarcity out to be an ubiquitous and permanent feature of the human condition.

The etymological roots of the word 'scarcity' go back to the Old Northern French word *escarcte* which meant insufficiency of supply. Until the late 19th century, scarcity connoted a temporally bounded period of scarcity or a dearth. Scarcity was experienced cyclically, dependent usually on poor yields. After the industrial revolution which led to cataclysmic changes creating new needs, desires and the frustration of desires, the concept acquired a new meaning which culminated in its 'invention' in neo-classical economic thought of the 18th century [Xenos 1989: 7]. From scarcities, which were temporally bound and spatially differentiated, came the scourge of scarcity, 'a kind of open-ended myth' [ibid:35] from which deliverance was sought. Scarcity, not a scarcity or scarcities, was essentialised and its simplistic universalisation led to the obscuring of ambiguities and regional variations. In modernity, the elusive twin of scarcity is abundance, making scarcity 'the antagonist in the human story, a story with a happy ending; vanquishing of the antagonist and a life of happiness ever after and abundance for all' [ibid:35].

Deliverance from scarcity could only take place, philosophers argued, via progress. Shades of this are still found in theories of modernisation which promote unilinear paths from 'under-development' to 'development'. Progress became the focus for social critics such as Marx and Mill whose theories argued that abundance was the prerequisite for the full realisation of human capacities. These models continue to be 'evoked today by those who take refuge in the hope of an abundant future to assuage their sense of the injustices of present-day scarcity' [ibid:36].

In the international discourse on water resources management, water scarcity is taken to be a given and starting point for policy agendas [Postel 1994]. Until very recently, the supply-oriented nature of water resources management focused on meeting the ever-growing and competing needs of industry, agriculture and domestic use. The perversity of these needs, for example, growing water-guzzling sugar cane in times of droughts or prioritising cement plants over drinking water schemes, is rarely questioned in state discourse. Even the recent demand-oriented notion of water as an 'economic good' does not question the uni versalised notion of water scarcity [e.g., Winpenny 1994]. From being a 'free-good' pillaged by free-riders, water is converted into an 'economic good' that needs to be managed by dam builders and water bureaucrats.

It would be an ontological fallacy to deny that there is no such thing as water scarcity or water shortage. The ever-increasing length of time spent by women on water collection and the visible decline of groundwater reserves in aquifers are clear indications of one aspect of the problem of water scarcity. There are, however, many other intangible and ambiguous aspects of the problem leading to different types of scarcities felt by a wide range of actors. Hence the responses to 'scarcity' are also varied and there is need to understand their relational aspects. Over and above the understanding of the tangible and physical evidences of the problem (i.e., dwindling water levels), the paper also seeks to understand what scarcity means for different actors. The focus is also on how certain actors in Gujarat have constructed a naturalised and essentialised notion of scarcity. In doing so, I follow Yappa's urgent plea to 'include the very intellect that helped us to conceptualise' the problem in the first place [Yappa 1993:225].

Case of Kutch

The crescent-shaped peninsula of Kutch is the largest district in Gujarat and has an area of 45,612 sq km constituting 23 per cent of the state. Kutch is like an island as it is bound by the sea to the south and west and by the 'Ranns' (salt marshlands) in the east and north. It has nine talukas or administrative sub-districts: Bhuj and Nakhatrana in the north; Lakhpat and Abrasa in the west; Mandvi, Mundra and Anjar in the south and Bachau and Rapar in the east. Apart from its very heterogeneous social and ethnic composition, the region has nine ecological zones [Gujarat Ecology Commission 1994].

Kutch has an arid to semi-arid type of climate. Temperatures range from 45 degrees centigrade in the summer to two degrees in winter. Humidity and evapo-transpiration are high throughout the year. In some areas, groundwater supplies are abundant, but increasingly the levels are dropping. Over-exploitation of the aquifer combined with sea water ingression has led to salinity in the water and soils and a sinking water table. The groundwater table sinks at a rate of a metre a year and, in two talukas in the district, falls under the over-exploitation category [Gujarat Ecology Commission 1994:14].

Rainfall is erratic and variable and averages about 350 to 370 mm. There is high regional variation, ranging from 440 in southern Kutch to 338 mm in western Kutch [Raju 1995: 10]. It only rains a few days a year (15 on an average) with significant intra-district variations. In official discourse, Kutch is considered drought-prone, with droughts taking place every 2-3 years.

Scarcity conditions in Kutch are often attributed to dwindling rainfall [Mehta 2001]. However, this is a myth, both in Kutch as well as in other parts of the world [cf Falkenmark et al. 1990]. Rainfall data of the past 60 years prior to 1997 indicate that while there have been erratic variations in the quantity of rainfall, there is no evidence to suggest that precipitation rates have changed. A t-test, comparing the rainfall in Kutch over 30 years (1968-1997) with the previous 30 year period (1938-1967), revealed no significant difference (tob(. = -.28, p > 0.052.mil). Inference tests using rainfall data for the talukas of Abrasa, Bhuj and Rapar over a longer period (120 years) were conducted to compare rainfall differences between four 30-year periods (1878-1907, 1908-1937, 1938-1967 and 1968-1997). A repeated measures analysis of variance revealed no significant differences over these periods [Sinclair 1998].

Kutchi identity is moulded around water, or the lack of it. Villagers across the length and breadth of the district say that the lack of water is the cause of their misery, the depopulated villages and mass migration out of Kutch. Water scarcity is attributed to low rainfall, ever-decreasing rainfall and perennial droughts. There is a widespread belief in Kutch that due to the harsh climate, erratic water supply, declining groundwater sources and frequent droughts, the only solution is to get water from the rivers of Gujarat [Kutch Development Forum 1993]. That is why all hopes are being pinned on the Sardar Sarovar Project (SSP) which is also made out to be Gujarat's lifeline [Raj 1991]. It is also projected by many to be the only hope for Kutch.

Politics of Scarcity: Kutch and the Sardar Sarovar Project

Plans to provide water for Kutch from the river Narmada have a long history and are no less complicated than the history of the Sardar Sarovar dam itself. Though the project was conceived almost a century ago, actual work has been stalled due to interstate conflicts such as the height of the dam, the extent of submergence and the sharing of benefits. Different committees were set up to resolve all these interstate conflicts, including the Khosla Commission of 1965 and the Narmada Water Disputes Tribunal of 1979. Kutchis maintain that the government of Gujarat did not represent their interests adequately and was biased towards obtaining benefits for central Gujarat despite its more favourable water endowments. As a result, Kutch successively lost out in the several rounds of negotiations. From an original plan of three canals, the Narmada Water Disputes Tribunal sanctioned only the canal along the coast in 1979. Instead of allowing for the irrigation of 9.45 lakh acres of land in Kutch, only 95,000 acres of land were to get irrigation [Kutch Development Forum 1993]. In this way less than 2 per cent of Kutch's area stands to benefit from the Kutch Branch Canal.

The hurdles of the past, however, are few compared with future chances of getting water to the region. Water can only enter Kutch after the Narmada main canal is constructed. Once diverted into the main canal, the water will traverse 500 kilometres before it enters into Kutch. Along the way the canal will cross major rivers such as the Mahi, the Sabarmati and the Banas and their valleys. Before entering Kutch, it will also cross the Little Rann. Here high evaporation is expected. The quantum of water entering into Kutch will almost be that of a small river. Consensus still has to be reached on whether the lift or gravity method will be used. No work has started as yet on the proposed Kutch Branch Canal (KBC) as the alignment line has not yet been fixed. The present plan envisages a canal of 200 kilometres in Kutch passing through a tiny coastal strip in eastern and southern Kutch. In this way five talukas stand to benefit: Rapar, Bachau, Anjar, Mundra and Mandvi. Only two of these talukas, namely Rapar and Bhachau, are considered to be drought-prone. The other three are richer in groundwater endowments and are considered to be part of the belt that has experienced the Green Revolution in Kutch. The industrial belt of Kutch in the Kandla-Gandhidham area is also located in the command area. Thus, the needs of industrial residents and rich farmers may be met more than those of needy farmers in other drought-prone areas. The SSP, if realised, may also intensify the existing class divide in the district. In short, the project of providing water from the SSP to Kutch continues to be embryonic and promises to be a protracted process. It is ironic that water-hungry Kutch should be used by the dam proponents to justify the project, given how unlikely it is that Kutch will benefit significantly from it. Recently a pipeline brought Narmada water to Samakhiyari village in Kutch, some 600 km north of the Sardar Sarovar dam. It remains to be seen whether work on the canals will continue and whether the dam will indeed assuage Kutch's water needs.

The propaganda machinery used by the state as well as decades of political promises have succeeded in 'manufacturing' perceptions or myths that reinforce the idea of SSP as bounty. In their book *Manufacturing Consent,* Herman and Chomsky describe the role of the media in mobilising support for the special interests that dominate the state activity. In Gujarat, the state has manufactured one dominant perception of water scarcity, namely, the Narmada project as the magic bullet. In doing so, political and business interests all over the state are being served. Additionally, the discourse on water resources management is overwhelmed by this one project. The focus on externally-supplied water has prevented water-harvesting schemes from gaining widespread acceptance in Gujarat. Officials of the Gujarat State Land Development Corporation (GSLDC) feel that their work is marginalised in water resources departments in Kutch and in Gandhinagar. Their efforts are stymied due to the statewide obsession with the Narmada project. An official of the GSLDC in Bhuj said:

If all the 177 watersheds in Kutch would be developed, there would be no need for Narmada water. But our work is not taken seriously. Everybody is obsessed with the Narmada project, but what should the people do until the water comes? We lack human power, our offices are understaffed and during scarcity years, all our work comes to a standstill because our schemes are converted to relief sites. In areas where we have worked, wells have been recharged and water conservation has increased. The need for relief has gone down. But this is a long and protracted process, which cannot take place overnight.

Villagers in the research village also echo these sentiments. Every year they watch helplessly as water flows unchecked into the Rann due to Kutch's topography. Due to the sharp gradient, all the 97 rivers and streams of Kutch are non-perennial and have a high run-off rate. The limited rainfall flows off in streams and rivulets into the sea or the Ranns. Thus there is great potential for rainwater harvesting and catchment area treatment. However, in the late 1990s, Kutchis had largely bought into the grand narrative of SSP as a 'water wonder'. They felt that it would solve all their problems and make up for the injustices of climate and history, especially the trail of broken promises made by politicians. The widespread 'manufactured' nature of debates around the SSP also helped obscure the anthropogenic nature of scarcity to which I now turn.

Anthropogenic Dimensions of Scarcity

While the actual volume of rainfall might not have changed,

the severity of drought or scarcity is felt more acutely today than in the past. Scientists and local people maintain that the intensity of drought has increased [cf Murishwar and Fernandes 1988]. There are several factors at play. The first factor is increasing devegetation which has certainly occurred due to increased commercial logging in the last five decades. Prior to Kutch's integration into the Indian Union, the Maharaos had instituted a policy of afforestation. Areas known as 'rakhals' were set aside, where tree cutting and grazing were prohibited. The rakhals were used as game sanctuaries, grass farms and for experiments at reforestation. Despite their elitist nature, the rakhals succeeded in experimenting with the types of trees suitable for Kutch's unique requirements and considerable forest cover was created [Rushbrook Williams 1958: 29]. After 1948, institutional restrictions on rakhals ceased to exist and there was a boom in unchecked logging. Cut trees were smuggled out of Kutch into Gujarat for coal, resulting in serious loss of vegetational cover. The wild growth of 'ganda bawal' ('*Prosopis juliflora*') has also led to loss of grass cover and the undermining of indigenous tree species. Moreover, it is believed that *ganda bawal* neither attracts rain nor gives moisture to the soil even though it might conserve water within its own system. Bad water management practices have also played a role in vegetational reduction. The world famous grasslands in northern Kutch, for example, have suffered considerably due to the damming of Kutch's northern rivers. The damming stopped the annual inundation and natural fertilisation by the silt traditionally brought by the rivers. The grasslands are now dependent only on rainfall for their rejuvenation [Ferroukhi 1994:41].

Another dimension to anthropogenic scarcity is the over-exploitation of groundwater aquifers. Access to and control over groundwater in Kutch is marked by tremendous inequality. In my research village, higher castes such as the Rajputs and Jadejas comprise less than 30 per cent of the population but they control about 65 per cent of the land. They also own most of the wells in the village. Well ownership goes hand in hand with land ownership. Those who have access to land, control the water below them. The rich irrigators in rural areas (popularly known as 'water lords') are often responsible for depleting vast amounts of groundwater resources. They tend, however, to attribute declines in the groundwater to climatic change which again obfuscates the real problem: namely, rapidly increasing groundwater use [cf Olsen 1987]. This can only dry out local wells and ponds and has far-reaching effects on biomass regeneration and the water recharging capacity of soils. Clearly, water extraction exceeds water recharging. Consequently, the water table is declining by about one metre every year in Kutch. Groundwater is Kutch's most precious, yet, most abused resource. Its control lies in the hands of powerful landed owners and irrigators for whom it is the most important form of material capital in their local communities [Shah 1993]. These water lords overcome groundwater constraints by their willingness and financial ability to invest in annual or even monthly well digging, broadening and deepening operations. They are also successful at circumventing legislation and making the best of institutional loopholes. The groundwater crisis, hence, is not just one of dwindling water levels, but instead a crisis of access and control over scarce resources. Irrigators in the region often tend to think short-sightedly. This manifests itself in their willingness to tap scarce water resources during droughts to grow water-hungry crops as the next sections demonstrate.

The above discussion should make it clear that the growing water 'crisis' in Kutch is largely human-induced. However, in popular discourse, the anthropogenic dimension of water scarcity is obscured. The culpability of large farmers, bad water management practices and state policies is denied. The story of 'dwindling rainfall' obscures the fact that water has been misused and regulations constantly circumvented. The power of the water lords remains unquestioned and their greed is exonerated. The water problem is seen as 'natural', something beyond human agency, even though rainfall and drought patterns are characterised by high uncertainty and variability. Projects such as the SSP are evoked as the only solution to set right what nature has ostensibly disturbed.

Differentiated Responses to Scarcity

I now turn to village level experiences of water scarcity by drawing on findings from a village which I call Merka in eastern Kutch. The village is situated in the potential command area of the SSP. It is a medium-sized village with a population of 3,463. It has been declared a 'no source' village by the state which means that existing water supplies in the village are not sufficient to provide water to its population. Water is, thus, supplied by the Gujarat Water Supply and Sewage Board either by tanker or by pipeline.

Merka is a multi-caste village. Caste is the basis for most social interactions and also plays a crucial role in local water resources management practices. Merka's castes range from the erstwhile feudal lords (jadejas) to rajputs (warrior castes), pastoralists (rabaris, bharvads) and dalits (scheduled castes). Sources of water comprise tanks around the village where rainwater is collected, wells with groundwater and 'virdas', holes in the riverbed (see Mehta forthcoming for details on caste politics and water).

In rural Kutch, the outcome of every year is uncertain. Periods of abundance are interspersed with periods of dearth and impoverishment. Rainfall is largely characterised by uncertainty and can be seen to be 'regularly irregular'. What are the institutional arrangements that deal with this uncertainty and scarcity? Livelihood strategies display a high degree of flexibility. Let me begin with dryland agriculture and pastoralism and the links between the two.

Dryland agriculture employs a wide range of risk minimisation strategies such as the spreading of land assets over different land parcels distributed over a variety of soil types. Decision-making regarding field preparation is often an innovative response to an ever-changing environment. For example, if villagers sense a lean year, they are likely to plant drought-hardy crops. If the year appears promising, they invest in millet or cotton. Crop-related decisions are not just dependent on exogenous factors such as the rainfall. Personal need, practicalities and collegiality towards field neighbours are also important factors. Thus, agricultural practices are flexible responses to situations at a given time and given place. They are adaptations to the year, particular soil conditions and to highly specific contingencies arising within the social world. For example, it is usual to confer with field neighbours and collectively negotiate on crops to be grown in a particular vicinity. To borrow Paul Richards' useful analogy, all these factors make agriculture in Kutch an ongoing performance which is a 'sequential adjustment to unpredictable conditions' [Richards 1989: 41]. Clearly of course, not all cultivators have uniform strategies. Large landowners with irrigation facilities enjoy the maximum buffer against uncertainty. By contrast, dryland cultivators and marginal farmers face the knocks of scarcity more.

The same resource base is also used by herders, since the livestock-based economy has always been one of the most important sources of livelihood in Kutch. The district's semi-arid to arid type of climate encourages a vegetation of short annual grasses ideal for livestock rearing. The pastoralists are usually sedentary but, during lean years, the uncertainty of rainfall and forage availability in the village environs makes migration necessary. Those with large herds can afford to migrate for about 400 kilometres. Migration thus allows pastoralists with large herds to adapt to a variable and heterogeneous environment. Due to this mobility they can exploit and access different social and ecological patches across the range. One always hopes, quite literally, that the grass is greener on the other side. Each site has its own set of forage opportunities and restrictions. The water situation is always different, as is the reception from the host community. The institutional arrangements need to be highly flexible and entail constant decisions that respond to unexpected contingencies. Those with fewer animals (under 100) cannot afford to migrate and have to make do with locally available grasses.

Migratory pastoralism is possible only due to the wide support and social networks spread out over a wide area, indicating the embeddedness of institutions in wider social structures. These social networks include kinship ties amongst other pastoralists but also reciprocal relationships with farmers that have been built over several generations. The relationship between cultivators and pastoralists who use the same resource base has largely been synergistic. Landowners appreciated the manure provided by the pastoralists and they were allowed to pitch camp on fallow or harvested fields during their migratory routes. Recently, however, changes in agricultural patterns have made the relationship less symbiotic, with pastoralists losing out. State policies and interventions have tended to offer agricultural subventions to cultivators, leading to the introduction of double and triple cropping. The migration of pastoralists is actively discouraged with pastoralists being fined or areas being sealed off. Kutch has no state policies that foster pastoralists' rights to pastures. The diverse ways in which different resource users use the same land and CPR resources is not appreciated. The institutional flexibility displayed by cultivators and pastoralists as they adapt their livelihoods to deal with uncertainty has been undermined, leading to a general worsening of ties between the two groups.

Of course, the diversity in livelihood strategies in drought-prone Merka is also shaped by people's occupational status and wealth assets. I now explore two different households' experiences of drought in 2000 in the course of a three year drought cycle. I focus on a rich irrigator family with 100 acres of land and a labouring family with 5 acres of land.

Two Household Profiles

Raghubhai and his sons and their families live in a majestic old house with a large courtyard. Together they own about 100 acres of land (spread out across the village and under various names). The patriarch is one of the richest men in the village. About 20 acres of land are irrigated by four wells with saline water. Their prize is the 25 acres of land adjacent to a small check-dam from which they extract sweet water which they use to grow commercial crops such as cumin and castor. These activities have actively contributed to depleting the water in village communal tanks. Since this family is the patron of about twenty families spread out over the village in every quarter and caste, these activities do not meet with much resistance. The family has the financial clout to constantly deepen, broaden and extend their wells. This ensures good yields in a dry year.

The family grows subsistence crops such as bajra, mug and tal in fields all around the village. In addition they grow fodder crops such as lucerne and jowar on irrigated fields in the dry months. In this way their cattle are assured of fresh green fodder. Cotton and cumin are their chief cash crops, grown on irrigated land. In good years, they can make about Rs 4 lakhs with a profit of about Rs 2 lakhs. Cotton can grow with saline water from their wells. However, cumin cultivation is only possible with sweet water for which they use village communal tanks, often without permits.

This family does not suffer tremendously due to the drought. There is no change in their diet and milk continues to be drunk by all members, including women and girls. Even during the drought year of 2000-2001, the third year of the drought cycle, their large land assets and irrigation facilities ensured a modest yield (3,000 kilos of grain and cereal which would last a year and 4,000 kilos of cumin). They somewhat managed to break even against their initial investment of Rs 2.5 lakhs. Drought for this family means fewer yields and fewer profits which mean not having the cash to build a house or celebrate a wedding. In no way does drought entail misery or loss.

By contrast, drought means debt, hardship and a somewhat reduced intake of milk and milk products for the household of Kasiben and Khimjibhai, two dalits. They have eight children and earn most of their money through seasonal labour and cultivation. Khimjibhai's father's land is shared between four brothers. It is so insignificant that Khimjibhai considers himself, for all practical purposes, to be landless. Against a payment of Rs 10,000, the family acquired land from a pauperised darbar which they now cultivate in partnership with him. They have two parcels of land—one is near the Rann and the other is close to one of the dams of the village.

They usually grow cotton and castor in one field and grains and cereals in another. In a good year, they can harvest about 400 kilos of grains and cereals. They keep about eight months' worth and sell the rest. Unlike Raghubhai, their surpluses are not stored and no seeds are stored. Buying seeds can be difficult following a drought year. When the season is favourable they can earn about Rs 40,000 a year from agricultural activities, largely from cotton sales. In a bad year, their yields are very limited and last for barely a month or so. In 1995, Khimjibhai borrowed money (interest-free) from Raghubhai. In 2000, the three consecutive years of drought had taken their toll and Kasiben had pledged her jewellery to the moneylender against a loan of Rs 6,000.

In 2000-2001, they reported that the first two rains were good but the last crucial shower failed. Hence the entire year was disappointing and there was no hope of any profits, but Khimjibhai felt that he would break even. They also could not irrigate one of their fields near the dam because Raghubhai's family used up all the water in the tank. Since their relationship is one of patronage and dependence, they could not afford to be overtly critical.

The effects of drought are far more pronounced on this family and the periods of dearth are more extreme than for the large farmers. During drought periods, the pernicious trap of being indebted to the money-lender is a constant worry, the intake of milk produce is drastically decreased and the dependence on casual labour and relief is strong. But even this family does not compromise on food intake during the drought. They continue to eat pulses, grains and vegetables, largely purchased from the shop. Clearly, without relief work and other employment opportunities this dalit family would encounter far more deprivation than it does currently.

These household profiles demonstrate two things: One, livelihood and drought-coping strategies in Merka are quite diverse and adaptable. Two, they are highly dependent on wealth and assets which explains the vast differences between the two families. Three, there is a high correlation between wealth and security. Secure livelihoods are maintained by large farmers who also have irrigation facilities which they enjoy, often to the detriment of poorer households' well being. For example, their over-exploitation of the water in the communal tanks prevents the poor in the village from enjoying a minimum level of irrigation. By contrast, the dalit family with its meagre assets experiences high insecurity. Their dependence on state-sponsored relief measures is very high. Thus, scarcity and drought mean different things to different resource users and their experiences and perceptions are largely linked with people's wealth, assets and social positioning.

I experienced drought in Merka in 1995-96 which was a semi-scarcity year and in 2000, at the end of the three year drought cycle. In 2000 Merka's rainfall was better than the Kutchi average and those with irrigation facilities were not doing too badly. But the three years of drought had visible manifestations: unlike in 1995-96, people clearly seemed to be weighed down by fodder scarcity, low agricultural yields, debts and problems with ganda bawal. They also complained about the lack of liquid cash flow and few or no off-farm employment facilities.

But, the relative normalcy of drought, no matter how difficult and hard, was also evident. In response to my questions about drought, people would laugh:

"We are used to drought. Two years are bad and one year is good. This is our life. When it's bad we disappear away from the village. When the rains come, we race back. This is our home and we are happy here".

But this acceptance of the cyclical nature of drought and scarcity may not always persist. Even the highly adapted, flexible and diverse livelihood strategies of both cultivators and pastoralists will not always be able to withstand the problems of dwindling groundwater aquifers, depleted vegetation, and soil degradation. There are limits to local resilience. I do not want to overly glorify 'adapting to and living with scarcity and uncertainty'. However understanding their dynamics will help planners and policy-makers overcome their 'dryland blindness' [Mehta 2000] and promote interventions that contribute to mitigating scarcity, instead of naturalising it.

Largely, planners have not built on local people's coping strategies vis-a-vis scarcity. Instead of promoting dryland agriculture or agro-pastoralist occupations, they have neglected them. They do not view scarcity as a temporally bound phenomenon. Instead, Kutch is made out to be permanently drought-prone and cursed by scarcity. State-sponsored water interventions have not succeeded in mitigating scarcity. In fact, some of them have exacerbated the water problems in certain areas, making scarcity indeed ever-present and all-pervasive. These flawed interventions arise because of the prevailing world-views and experiences of policy-makers—their dryland blindness—and because of institutional weaknesses in water management programmes. At one level, the people of Kutch imagine and experience scarcity as something that is cyclical, periodic and part of their lives. Increasingly, however, scarcity has become naturalised and all-pervasive, due to a tors. As long as this situation persists, scarcity and its accompanying 'scarcity and relief industry' will dominate life in Kutch.

4

Natural Resources Availability and Conflicts

At the largest of spatial scales, resources and conflict have long been a matter of geopolitics and struggles for the control of supplies of key materials. Oil in the Persian Gulf is the classic example that comes to mind from the period of the cold war. The contemporary focus on conflict in the Gulf and in Central Asia continues a pattern related to petroleum supplies. Whether one invokes the term 'resource war' or not, the relationships between violence and the supplies of vital materials are a persistent part of the pattern of international rivalries. The extension of the national interest to outside national borders to ensure the supply of essential materials turns defence into intervention, national security into imperial ambition.

This is not a novel argument. In a more technocratic mode, similar themes were part of the debate about the limits to growth in the early 1970s and in the aftermath of the 'oil crisis' of 1973 and 1974. That scarce resources were a cause of conflict was accepted as common sense in the World Commission on Environment and Development and in much of the literature that followed. In the light of rising concern about ozone holes, climate change, droughts, tropical forest decline in the late 1980s in North America and Europe, these arguments appeared in the terms of a discussion of 'environmental security'. Environmental degradation might, some argued, become a cause of warfare as scarcity drove desperate people to fight for the remaining resources.

The assumption that environmental degradation might cause conflict and, on the largest scale, warfare between states, became an important part of the discussion of security after the demise of the cold war. It triggered considerable scholarly debate and empirical research in various places but, despite numerous case studies, arguments continue about both the relationships between environment and conflict and whether these issues are usefully discussed in terms of environmental security. In the 'environmental security' debate, the empirical link between environmental change and violence was more often assumed than demonstrated. It was also assumed that linking the environment and conflict in this manner was a suitable focus for policy prescription.

The dominant formulations of these matters in the north in the last decade have drawn on fears of conflict over scarce resources to formulate interventionist policies. In some cases, fears of spreading conflict have been used to formulate policies that focus on the stability of particular states as a foreign policy on the part of the US. While at first glance, and viewed from the affluently appointed office suites of policy-makers in Washington, the term environmental security seems eminently sensible, once one probes a little into its conceptual assumptions, the construction of environment in terms of security quickly becomes problematic. It also, not surprisingly, becomes the site of a political argument about the nature of threats and precisely who is insecure and why. Critics have forcefully argued that using concerns about security to raise alarm about deleterious environmental trends in many places has not necessarily produced appropriate policy thinking. Neither environment nor security, it turns out, is simple; neither can be invoked without terminological and political difficulties. Juxtaposing these compounds the difficulties although it presents interesting possibilities for critiquing both.

Discussions of environment and security are ineluctably part of the larger constructions of geopolitics, and as such need to be examined in this discursive context. The argument in what follows emphasises the large-scale geographical premises of the environmental security discourse. It is possible to analyse all this in terms of critical linguistic approaches to political discourse as has been done elsewhere. It is also relatively easy to trace its historical antecedents in terms of the two-century-old debate about Malthus. Both of these themes appear below, but in what follows I look more specifically at the taken-for-granted context-ualisations of the debate, the usually unquestioned geographies in the discourse. These geographical specifications of security are usually unquestioned because they appear to be so obvious. To rethink the modern assumptions of autonomy, separation and threat on which security discourse operates, requires, in Alfred North Whitehead's terms from the epigraph to this paper, 'unusual minds'. Such rethinking also requires revisiting the historical legacy of empire and its reinvention in the current patterns of global urbanisation.

Environment and Conflict

In reading the literature on environmental security that has appeared in the past 15 years, basically since the publication of the Brundtland Report, a number of themes have become clear. The initial policy discussion took it for granted that environmental degradation was a widespread problem, and that it was one that post-cold war security planners ought to take seriously. The social science literature has long suggested that matters are much more complex, but that has not stopped the repeated reinvention of discourses of environmental threat. Nonetheless, as the debate has progressed, the calls to examine the complexity of the issues and to investigate specific contexts have become more prominent.

First, there was an initial concern to identify environment as a threat in terms that were broadly similar to the formulations of cold war security discourse. Whether this was in the US, or in the Soviet Union, where environmental security became a matter of considerable importance in the final years of the Gorbachev administration, instabilities and disruptions to society as a consequence of environmental problems were the dominant theme. Once again, external threats to the political order of modernity structured the discussion; policies determined at the centre would monitor and hopefully contain threats.

Second, there was a substantial literature in social science trying to formulate an appropriate empirical validation of the basic contention that environmental matters cause social threats. Thomas Homer-Dixon's teams of researchers, who became known as the Toronto school, posited a series of complex links between environmental scarcities and social responses which, "when coupled to other political factors such as weak states with inadequate capacities for resource management, appropriate infrastructure provision or conflict resolution, would likely lead to overt conflict". Homer-Dixon's attempts to construct matters in conventional American social science terms or, more specifically, to establish a plausible series of causal links between environmental scarcity and conflict, met with objections from other scholars who charged that the case was made on the basis of highly selective case studies. Calls for comparison cases and null hypotheses appeared in the pages of scholarly journals and books.

Third, in Europe, the Swiss Peace Federation sponsored a large project, which included several case studies, looking at violence and environment in various places. Drawing on more broadly conceived intellectual traditions than the empirical methods of North Americans, the ENCOP project linked environmental conflicts to development problems and the spreading influence of commercial societies. Most explicitly, Gunther Baechlerdrew on Karl Polanyi's formulations of The Great Transformation to suggest that poverty-ridden marginal lands in mountainous regions and more remote areas of Africa on the margins of ecological zones were the most likely locations for environmental conflict. But there were other dimensions to the relation of environment and conflict too, not least the damage done to specific environments and local peoples by the dislocations of major development projects. The struggles by indigenous peoples to protect rainforests and other lands from oil wells and mining corporations are part of this larger pattern.

Fourth, in the late 1990s, the environmental scarcity leading to conflict argument, and neo-Malthusianism more generally, was tackled quite directly by some researchers interested in the emergent research in political ecology. Challenging the work of Robert Kaplan, and some of Thomas Homer-Dixon's earlier arguments, the political ecology literature focused much more on the political economy of resources and, in particular, the complexity of local resources intersecting with the global commercial economy. Showing how local power structures, gendered access to farm land, traditional modes of subsistence agriculture and fishing were overlain with new modes of resource extraction, this literature challenged the arguments about scarcity in the neo-Malthusian formulations. Although some of the authors might be guilty of too hastily dismissing Homer-Dixon's arguments, and especially of overlooking the importance of 'structural scarcity', 'resource capture' and 'ecological marginalisation' as crucial parts of the sequence that frequently leads to violence, what this critical literature has made very clear is that the complexities of the global economy have to be factored into local struggles, and that this has to be done with considerable care to ensure that the specifics of local circumstances are incorporated into the analysis.

Fifth, in the late 1990s, an apparent counter-argument suggested that resource shortages were not correlated with conflict. The converse, it was suggested, was the case. More specifically, the argument emerged that 'greed' rather than 'grievance' was the motivation behind some of the persistent and violent conflicts in the poorer parts of the world. Civil wars were clearly tied into the struggle to control the rents from resource streams that were being exported to the global economy. Controlling resources, whether timber, diamonds or oil, was the way to get rich quick, rather than follow the painful and slow routes of economic development. Elite rivalries and the promise of wealth are, so goes the argument, powerful incentives to initiate hostilities, especially where tribal or other particularistic loyalties can be mobilised. But these wars were not largely about either subsistence lands or the politics of agriculture. They might overlap with the politics of marginal populations that concerned some of the ENCOP researchers, but the resources that were in some cases the cause of the fighting were 'lootable' and hence easily removed and smuggled or traded illegally.

The discussion of these contemporary resource wars in some ways connects back to earlier debates on resources and conflict, but the link to contemporary civil wars also connects to the larger matters of development, failed states and the international political economy of the arms trade. The links between resources, environments and conflict are clearly numerous, and their construction in political and academic discourse is unlikely to follow any single formulation. Nor is there any reason to think that conflict and resources can be connected by a unidirectional causation.

Question of Definition

The sheer diversity of terrestrial contexts in which conflict might occur, and the multiplicity of materials that might be considered resources by many diverse cultures and economies, make generalisation very difficult. More complex still are the ecological contexts within which environmental conflict supposedly occurs. Work in Africa suggests that at least some of the environmental changes that have alarmed observers in recent decades are cyclical fluctuations rather than signs of irreversible human destruction. Simple degradation explanations frequently do not take history or ecological complexity into account, nor the specifics of particular environments, much less the micro-level contestations of property relations, gender and cultures that are crucial to explaining either crises or everyday practices.' But empirical generalisation is precisely what social science promises to provide and what policy-makers seek in justifying various courses of action.

The early literature assumed that conflicts occur due to the absence of supplies of key resources. Michael Klare has updated the argument recently in his suggestions about likely scenarios for future conflicts. Besides oil, scarce water is the focus of conflict in a number of situations, not least the west Asia where many studies have examined both the potential for conflict and the possibilities of peacemaking as a result of cooperative arrangements for resource management. On the other hand, the counter-argument that resource wars focus on abundance and struggles for control over resource rents suggests that the opposite situation is more 'likely to cause conflict. Abundance is understood here as the problem, not scarcity.

But a few moments' reflection on these contentions, and especially the implicit assertion that they are by definition mutually exclusive, suggests both that matters are not well defined and that questions of the appropriate scales and contexts have been ignored. Resources are not just resources; renewables and non-renewables have different qualities. Contexts matter too; the exploitation of oil reserves is different in many ways from the use of marginal farmland. Subsistence activities are likely to have different social dynamics from the large-scale commercial exploitation of mineral raw materials. These matters need to be clarified if the debate about the environmental causes of conflict is to offer useful generalisations.

Thomas Homer-Dixon's analysis suggested that scarcities were a factor in political violence, but did not assert that all scarcities were alike or that all caused political violence. He deliberately set aside the notion of security because it was ill-defined; acute violence is easier to identify than insecurity. While Homer-Dixon's models are complex, his focus is on supplies of agricultural land and water, the basic ingredients of food production. He concluded that environmental violence was likely to be small scale, diffuse and mostly on a sub-national scale albeit with the ever-present possibilities of international dimensions where displaced populations crossed state boundaries. He pointed clearly to the importance of structural scarcities, situations where elites used a crisis to increase their control of resources and so marginalise further the poor and dispossessed. He also argued that control over resources in the urbanising slums of southern states pits newly arrived migrants against established residents within the same ethnic or national groups, leading to intra-ethnic disputes rather than ones that polarise on prior allegiances. Gunther Baechler's analysis suggested that marginal populations close to major ecotones were especially vulnerable and likely to end up in conflict situations as the pressure of numbers and expanding modern property arrangements pitted nomads and farmers against each other in the grasslands of Africa and in more remote mountainous areas where traditional cultures and ways of life are interacting with encroaching modernity.

On the other hand, the argument that resource abundance is likely to cause violence is obviously valid in some cases. Violence in Nigeria is related to the complex politics of oil extraction and the disruption of Ogoni environments where the local population does not reap any of the benefits of oil wealth. As the scriptwriters for the James Bond film 'Die Another Day' have noted, smuggled diamonds from conflict areas are part of global politics. Violence is related to the control of diamonds, gold and many other minerals. It is certainly part of the history and current politics of the exploitation of petroleum. But the definitional issue here is important. It is possible to argue that these resources are being fought over because they are scarce; they are, by definition, a resource precisely because they are not ubiquitous. And yet the violence is happening in places close to their production; its mine sites, oil-wells, pipelines and export routes that are geographically proximate to the conflicts. It is precisely these facilities where the resource is geographically abundant that are the location of military activity.

There is a simple matter of scale here that needs to be worked into the picture because both abundance and scarcity are part of any political economy; diamonds would not be valuable if they existed in all soils and were available to all by the simple expedient of using a shovel for a few minutes. If there is violence over the control of oil supplies where these are abundant, it is because they are in demand, hence relatively scarce, elsewhere. But conflicts have specific geographies in places where modernity is less established than in the more peaceful parts of the world where the resources exported from the conflict zones are consumed. Many of the weapons, and some of the funds to keep warfare going, do come from these distant places. If the geography of warfare ever did, it now no longer conforms to simple matters of blocs and states. The political economy of violence in the 'new wars' of the post-cold war world spills over boundaries and frontiers, linking resources and diasporic communities through complex long-distance political economies.

Scarcity, Abundance and Scale

The question of scarcity and scale is crucial here. The suggestions in both the Toronto model and the ENCOP framework are that marginal populations are vulnerable and that struggles may turn violent in local situations. The scale here is local, although of course displaced populations may have disruptive consequences far from the initial sources of scarcity. But it is clear that there is more than a simple notion of Malthusianism at work in these writings. In some places the scarcity of agricultural land, water supplies and pasture is aggravating the political tensions that plague marginal populations. Problems of what Baechler calls 'maldevelopment' or, in a closely analogous way, 'structural scarcity' in Homer-Dixon's schemes, are related to violence, especially in situations where states are not capable of effective government that resolves property and rural power issues.

Indeed, and this point is important in the ENCOP formulations of the causal pathways from environment to conflict, in many cases the imposition of centralised state resource projects often , either cause or aggravate matters precisely because of the forms of property enclosure involved which dispossess subsistence farmers and disrupt nomadic modes of living. Structural scarcity, in Homer-Dixon's terms, is enhanced as marginal populations lose their access to subsistence. The neat lines of property and park boundaries that are the modern state's mode of rendering problems legible and manageable frequently cause disruption and resistance that is then defined as environmentally-caused violence. Nonetheless, the fact that environmental disruptions are sometimes related to political violence seems unavoidable. But so too does the conclusion in both the Toronto school and the ENCOP analyses that this violence is likely to be sub-national and diffuse.

Clearly, abundance and scarcity are geographically as well as politically located. In this sense, the 'abundance or scarcity' as a source of violence argument is misconceived. Both are clearly related to violence in some circumstances; but the issue is under what circumstances and at which geographical scale. It is not clear that the forms of violence and the political arrangements that lead to polarisation, mobilisation and overt conflict are necessarily likely to be similar; the literature on the new resource wars suggests that overt violence in the form of civil war may result from competing attempts to gain control over resource rents. There is little evidence of an exactly analogous form of violence in the case of struggles over agricultural land or nomadic grazing lands. In the case of some commercially exported foodstuffs, and shrimp 'farms' may be the best example, violence is related to the export trade and dispossession of traditional uses of land and water are involved; but the case studies of this issue do not suggest violence on the scale of civil wars analogous to diamonds in Sierra Leone, timber and oil in Angola or oil in the Sudan.

Indeed, attention to the ecological and political-economic specificities suggests that environmental security is not an appropriate way to think about resource wars at all. Clearly, in so far as minerals and petroleum are not 'environmental', in the sense of being renewable parts of active current ecosystem processes, they can be excluded from discussions of environmental matters as a cause of conflict. But their extraction and, crucially, their consumption, has environmental consequences that may be disruptive of ecosystem processes both in terms of local effects and at the biospheric scale. Environmental disruptions are part of modernisation; the removal of populations in the way of dams, highways and other infrastructure, not to mention parks, game reserves and golf courses for tourists, is part of the process of urbanisation and the expansion of commercial modes of economy into rural societies. Violent opposition to such changes is not unusual; those who face dispossession are not always likely to appreciate all the benefits of urban progress.

Constructing the relation between violence and resources thus needs a much more nuanced geographical imagination to incorporate the general assertions of causality into the practical realities in different places. Abundance and scarcity may be concepts that matter in terms of discussing the largest scale and the most abstract dimensions of the human condition.

But practical relevance to either detailed scholarly research, or policy advice for states or international agencies, requires a much more specific focus on particular contexts and the geographical connections between resource extraction and exports to the urban markets of the global economy. But only some of these resources are 'renewable' and, strictly then 'environmental'.

Water Wars?

The causal link between environmental scarcity and political conflict is exemplified in the debate over water. It is widely claimed that water is the most obvious environmental resource over which conflict seems likely and that water wars will be the wars of the future. Supposedly, states vying for control over specific rivers will fight to secure access to supplies of fresh water. But once again, this hypothesis needs to be qualified by geographical specificity. In only a few cases are the strongest states located downstream on contested rivers. Both Israel and Egypt are in this situation. In 2002, Israel threatened Lebanon over the construction of water works on rivers that flow into Israel from Southern Lebanon. As Israel has long made clear, and as Palestinians aspiring to farm on the West Bank of the Jordan have repeatedly discovered to their cost, water is at a premium. In the case of Egypt, as Michael Klare argues, the state may well have a powerful incentive to promote subversion and civil dissent in Ethiopia to prevent the emergence of a developmental state and the building of dams on the Blue Nile in the upstream nation.

But empirical research into the matter suggests that, notwithstanding the few cases mentioned here, 'water wars' are rare and generally unlikely. Indeed, the research argues that cooperation is more likely in many cases as the benefits to all parties are clear. So too are the pitfalls of conflict that might destroy shared infrastructure essential to both sides. The contrasting case, in Michael Klare's discussion of Egyptian antagonism to Ethiopia, and the diversion of water supplies to irrigation projects in Ethiopia, emphasises that Ethiopian development itself is a danger to Egypt. But few states are so tied to the waters of one river that such extreme dynamics unfold. In the case of India and Bangladesh, a similar geography determines the potential conflict dynamics, but difficulties over water have usually generated bilateral cooperation despite security problems on other matters. Likewise Turkey, Iraq and Syria have considerable potential for conflict given the fact that the headwaters of the Tigris and Euphrates lie in eastern Turkey but flow into Syria and Iraq. Conflict here has been threatened, and tensions over Kurdish issues are sometimes intense, but overt hostilities concerning the Anatolia dam projects in Turkey have not broken out. In many other instances, the classic case being the Colorado in the southern US, upstream states are stronger and there is little the downstream state, in this case Mexico, can do about reduced water supplies. But note that, in the case of southwestern US, the conflict concerning the expropriation of water supplies has long been mainly within the US and about agricultural and urban appropriations at the cost of small-scale users and local ecologies.

The longer term possibilities of climate disruptions and environmental changes altering weather patterns and exacerbating shortages or excesses of water loom over these discussions. Greater precipitation in some places may in fact alleviate the potential for conflict by either increasing river flows and hence irrigation possibilities, or improving agricultural productivity by watering fields directly. It might also cause more unpredictable rainfalls and droughts. The important point here is that such variability will follow from 'global' consumption of carbon fuels and the production of greenhouse gases far more than they will flow from southern actions. Scarcities may be caused by actions far from the scene of the most acute political and economic disruptions. But while pollution is a huge problem in many places, especially in the growing cities of the south, it is rarely a direct cause of political conflict. There have been important exceptions, not least the struggles in eastern Europe in the 1980s where environmental destruction was a mobilising theme for opponents of Soviet rule.

Nonetheless, empirical discussions of environmental change and water repeatedly suggest that cooperation is far more likely in the case of water issues. A recent example of the attempts to resolve difficulties in the case of Lake Victoria suggests a stark alternative to the resource war scenarios. The need to curtail over-fishing and the importance of remediation has encouraged cooperation; scarcity leading to conflict arguments have not been common in the region and they have not influenced policy prescriptions. Indeed, following Jon Barnett's pointed argument, Canter and Ndegwa suggest that the Lake Victoria case bears out the criticism that the environment-conflict thesis 'is largely a conceptual lens invented by western analysts with particular northern security interests rather than empirical deductions'.

Imperial Formulations

But 'Lake Victoria' is in the middle of Africa! Which, given its name, just might suggest that imperial history matters in these discussions. If one stops and thinks about the relevant scale for discussing resource issues and conflicts in temporal terms rather than just in spatial terms then longer perspectives for thinking about resources and history have to be considered. More specifically, the violence in the 'wild zones' of the south can only be understood in a context that includes discussions of the legacies of imperialism. European imperialism had dramatic impacts on the natural ecologies of many parts of the globe that it touched. In Richard Grove's succinct summary:

"Colonial ecological interventions, especially in deforestation and subsequently in forest conservation, irrigation and soil 'protection', exercised a far more profound influence over most people than the more conspicuous and dramatic aspects of colonial rule that have traditionally preoccupied historians. Over the period 1670 to 1950, very approximately, a pattern of ecological power relations emerged in which the expanding European states acquired a global reach over natural resources in terms of consumption and then too, in terms of political and ecological control".

The processes of crop and animal introductions and the extension of the market in grains to a truly global market connected by railways and steamships produced a global division of production and globalised vulnerabilities to famine and poverty in a manner that led to the emergence of an underdeveloped third world by the early part of the 20th century. Economic arguments about comparative advantage were coupled to the naturalisation of disaster in the south as the product of a cruel nature to portray famine and political violence as a regrettable part of life for those who were unfortunate enough to not (yet) reap the benefits of European civilisation. The emergence of meteorology as a global monitoring system provided a form of knowledge that suggested the inevitability of famine and disaster in regions that were far from the European experience in many ways. Lack of civilisation on the part of non-Europeans could in part be explained by environmental matters; environmental determinism has long structured discussions of planetary politics in these terms; in this sense too much of the current debate is not new.

But in the 19th century, the expropriation of wealth from the south and the enrichment of the north in the process was sometimes also a matter of direct physical violence. Colonial wars were wars of conquest, as were the wars that Americans were involved in, despite their periodic claims to being an exceptional power not given to European-style colonial escapades. Not only were subject peoples forced into the commercial economy by the necessity to earn currency to pay the new European taxes, but their lands and resources were sometimes simply plundered. Violence in the attempts to control resources at the beginning of the 21st century in central Africa has been eerily prefigured by the violence of Belgian conquest, dispossession of native peoples and the wholesale looting of ivory and rubber in the 19th century. In this sense at least the resource wars of the contemporary period are all too familiar.

The geopolitical viewpoint, the view from the think-tanks in Washington and, all too often, from the academic classrooms in North America, is one of tame zones of prosperity threatened from without by spreading violence caused by indigenous environmental factors. This notion of wars in the periphery, as with their imperial predecessors over the last few centuries, relies on a geography that separates that periphery from the affluent civilisation. Instead of acknowledging imperial exploitation, northern policies promote modernisation, the taming of wilderness and the pacification of the uncivilised as bringing peace and prosperity in the long run for all. As Tuathail pithily puts the matter: "In sum, modern geopolitics is a condensation, of western epistemological and ontological hubris—an imagining of the world from an imperial point of view".

But, and this is the crucial point for thinking aflout how environment is constructed as a causal agent in discussions of conflict, imperial formulations of resources, markets and populations as matters for administration have frequently remained salient in the aftermath of formal decolonisation. Now that local political forces administer the parks, forests and rivers, the populations and their participation in commercial markets, the pattern of empire is reproduced in the supposedly post-colonial states. Calling these processes either development or globalisation invokes temporal or spatial designations that occlude the continuing importance of the patterns initiated centuries ago in the growth of European power. What are called effective states in current development discourse are all too frequently states that are effective at the extraction of resources for the global economy. The extraction of resources to fuel the global market, and the disruptions of local peoples and rural ecologies in the service of development follow an imperial pattern. This historical geography needs to be remembered. Its codification in numerous 'scientific' modes of resource evaluation, even its formulation of 'environment' as something potentially hostile in need of management, comes from this legacy of imperial knowledge.

More generally the historical pattern of development and the appropriation of resources is connected to the rapid urbanisation of humanity. The 20th century was notable for the huge expansion of population and its movement into urban areas. We are now an urban species and have wired and paved the planet to move food, timber, oil, electricity, minerals and all sorts of commodities from rural areas into these burgeoning cities. In a way loosely analogous to earlier imperial arrangements, the flow of commodities inevitably disrupts traditional forms of economic life. Just as wheat flowed from Africa to Rome so now does oil flew from the west Asia to other parts of the new imperium.

5

Features in Nature

Nature may exist outside society, but natural resources are social phenomena, composed of social investments that give nature social life.' Modernity has so invested nature with national identity that national maps now often appear to contain nature the way a Petrie Dish contains amoeba. But national maps do not describe nature's social geography; they rather represent modern territorialism impressing itself on nature; and territorialism is not the only social force invested in nature: mobility is equally important. Focusing more attention on mobility's investment in nature is critical as globalisation increases the power of mobility over natural elements, which begin their social life in national territory but may not stay there for long. Using only national maps to imagine geographies of natural resource environments blinds analysis in one eye.

To imagine better maps, we need to put geography in motion, to keep temporal as well as spatial dimensions in view. When we do, we see that natural resources live in social geographies defined simultaneously by mobility and territorialism. Natural things become natural resources in any one place only because social assets that make nature productive move in time and space. Globalisation expands the geographical scale of an old fact of life for natural resources, which begin their social life in places where people make territorial claims to nature, but live mostly in the realm of mobility, where all the social resources that combine to make nature productive move from hand to hand, place to place, and from one social identity to another.

Intersections of territorialism and mobility have shaped natural resource environments in south Asia since prehistoric times, and their conflicting cultural attachments animate old village communities and agrarian regions as well as modern cities and national states. The basic source of their conflict is this: people who live inside each enclosed territory enjoy proprietary authority over resources in that territory, which they invest to accumulate resources inside their own territory, while mobile folk move resources from one territory to another, to combine with local assets and to carry the proceeds away, back into the realm of mobility.

Over the centuries, transactions between mobile and territorial interests have expanded product chains and social wealth, but have also typically pitted mobile and territorial claims to resources against one another, as in classically fraught relations between nomads and farmers, between shifting and sedentary cultivators, and between merchants and artisans. A more complex but critical example of creative tension appears in histories of nationalism and globalisation: that is, in fraught interactions between mobile folk who bring separate territories under expansive, encompassing territorial authority, and local territorial folk who covet assets that move across wide spaces but also fight to maintain their own territorial order so they can put assets from the wider world to work on their own ground.

Combining productive powers and reconciling conflicting interests of territorialism and mobility became the speciality of elites who produced most historical records, who typically live in central territorial sites, spread their influence across networks of mobility, enrich themselves at intersections of territorialism and mobility, and endeavour to accommodate conflicting claims to resources with various combinations of coercion, adjudication, patronage, and persuasion. The geographical reach and provenance of resource elites has changed countless times, over centuries, and thus, their territorial domains have acquired many shifting, mobile geographies. In this light, we can say that in the long span of history, mobility has had the upper hand, overall, in transactions with territorialism.

From Mauryan times onward, mobile folk have repeatedly reshaped natural resource environments in southern Asia. In the second millennium of the Common Era, the spatial scale of mobility increased, as Turks, Afghans, Mongols, and Persians reshaped territories across Asia, as Europeans reshaped territories across the Americas, Africa, and Asia, and as mobile folk in south Asia reshaped territories across the subcontinent. By the 18th century, mobility made the fixing of boundaries in India quite imaginary, for as much as half the population may have then comprised mobile artisans and workers, peasants colonising new land, itinerant merchants, nomads, pilgrims, shifting cultivators, hunters, migratory service workers and literati, herders, transporters, soldiers, people fleeing war, drought, and flood, and camp followers supplying troops on the move. All this mobility entailed widespread conflict and a huge expansion of commercial activity, commodity production, and global interconnections.

In the 19th century, territorialism began its long march to modern dominance, and in south Asia, it marched with and against the British Empire. National state boundaries only covered the globe after 1950, however, and only then did all the histories of all peoples in the world, for all times, begin to appear inside our cookie-cutter world of national geography.

The force of mobility did not decline in the world of national maps, however. Declining transport costs, bigger populations, and increasing spatial inequality rather expanded its scale of operation. National boundaries now represent legal and cultural norms, but they do not contain mobility; they rather constitute modern instruments of power over mobility. Today, the new complexity of old tensions between mobility and territorialism appears most poignantly inside national territories, where people strive simultaneously to enforce the closure of their own territories, to control nature inside their own boundaries, to exclude and subdue aliens, to move in and out of territories, to bring in and take out resources, to move and settle in resource-rich places, to change and mix territorial identities, and to expand claims to resources in mobile territories like those defined by metropolitan regions, multinational corporations, and the US military.

To imagine more realistic geographies of natural resource environments than national maps provide, we can begin by abandoning the idea that territorialism could ever contain mobility. Territorial wealth and national development depend on mobility that territorialism cannot control, and mobility is always at work transforming territory in ways that territorialism does not com prehend. Thus it makes sense to locate studies of natural resource environments at geographical intersections of mobility and territorialism.

Locating Sylhet

Within a hundred mile radius of the city of Sylhet, in north-east Bangladesh, many territorial transformations have occurred over the centuries, in expansive geographies of mobility where people and resources have travelled widely and also combined locally in the social process of investing in nature. Sylhet city inhabits a mound of land in the floodplain of the Surma River. The city's immediate surroundings are as densely populated as any part of Bangladesh, but overall, the Sylhet region is much less densely populated than Bangladesh, at about 70 per cent the national figure, because it includes thinly populated mountains and lowlands that flood deeply and extensively for half of every year.

Sylhet inhabits nature-on-the-move. Tectonic shifts continue to lift the highlands and depress the deepest-flooding 'haor' basins. Natural gas moves underground in tectonic folds. Thumping earthquakes periodically destabilise water's established pathways. The Surma and the Kushiara define the Sylhet lowlands but are but the biggest of many moveable rivers descending from the mountains of Meghalaya, Tripura, Manipur, and Assam. Forty miles upstream from Sylhet town, the Surma and Kushiara split from the Barak. A hundred miles downstream, the Surma and Kushiara meander, split, and recombine before joining the Meghna, which then joins the Brahmaputra, whose main course shifted in the 1780s to send its confluence with the Meghna a hundred miles south.

All the lands around Sylhet were originally covered with dense jungle, broken only by rivers. Amidst massive annual flooding and the highest rainfall in south Asia, lowland societies have navigated this overflowing geography at strategic elevated sites, where inundated fields meet habitable land hacked out forests, above the flood. Nature's topography is thus a natural resource of enduring significance. Sylhet's town site typifies the lowlands by being partly natural and partly constructed. Eighteenth century District Records indicate that embankments that protected Sylhet town and farms around it were built, rebuilt, strengthened, and lengthened repeatedly to prevent the land washing away.

Sanctity marks many old sites of social investments on the land around Sylhet. Upriver in Cachar, a cult site for Kapilasram (or Siddheswar) retains the memory of an ancient river goddess who was eventually overshadowed by Siva. Such overlays occurred as migratory settlers transformed local territory, in the case of Kapilasram, as Bengali brahmans established Siva's local authority. In the Dimasa language of people in Cachar, 'Dimasa' means 'sons of the river', and Khasi people in nearby hills worship many river gods, among whom, goddess Kupli reigns supreme. Kapileswar perhaps came to life at an old Kupli cult site, where a social stratification of cult practices emerged as high caste settlers worshipped Siva, while other locals venerated the site but not Siva.

Kapilasram seems to encode the incorporation of an old Khasi locality by immigrant Siva-worshipping Bengalis. This cultural change would have been part of a very long, complex set of transformations. Like many other groups now called 'tribes', Khasis once occupied many sites in the lowlands, in their case, up the Ganga basin into Bihar and down to the old Ganga delta. Khasis settled there as specialists in shifting rice cultivation. Ancient Khasis pioneered rice farming in Vietnam's Red River delta, and when conquered by

Vietnamese, moved up the Red River, to Yunnan, China, and across northern Burma, into Assam and the Ganga basin. As Gangetic agrarian societies expanded their territorial domains eastward, from Mauryan times, people like the Khasis enriched Hindu cultures, but Gangetic territorialism also rested on the expansion of permanent farmland that forced all the Munda language speakers, including Khasis, to submit, assimilate, or move.

Over the centuries, lowland territorialism compelled and informed tribal territorialism in the uplands. In 1600, Koch, Khasi, Garo, and others still occupied many places in the lowlands, but facing unprecedented pressure to submit to the Mughals, most retreated to the mountains. After 1600 and again after 1800, the accelerated expansion of sedentary agriculture drove shifting cultivators out of the plains; it also increased violence between contending interests on the land, confined tribal societies to the hills, and produced new political forms in the mountains. All these connected trends continue today.

Siva' s overshadowing of the river goddess in Cachar represents one local moment in the advance of lowland territorialism, which produced Bengali societies on moving eastern frontiers of Gangetic cultures, by pushing permanent farms into places inhabited by shifting cultivators, who lived in the highlands and lowlands, who moved freely among forest and field, mountains and plains, and who hunted and fished without settling down permanently anywhere. Though mobile lifestyles remained well adapted to the environment's watery uncertainty, animist cults and non-Aryan practices, including matrilineal kinship, marked shifting cultivators as primitive aliens for the Hindu, Muslim, and European lowlanders who invested in nature inside expansive territories of sedentary agriculture, urbanism, state revenue, and permanent territorial authority.

Sylhet town (Srihatta) became a major centre of lowland territorialism after the 10th century CE. Before then, copper plate inscriptions indicate that land around the Kushiara was more densely populated, because Kamarupa kings had granted large tracts of land to immigrant brahmans and their supporting castes, to make this region part of Assam

(Khanda Kamarupa). In the 13th century, Afghans conquered Sena rajas, inducing more Hindus to move east into Sylhet, and Sylhet town's site on the Surma became a fortified centre for local rajas. In the 14th century, the town received the sanctity of Shah Jalal, who arrived from Turkestan with 300 'darvish', conquered local rajas, and introduced Islam. Ibn Batuta met Shah Jalal, in 1346, and described his commanding stature, ascetic celibacy, yogic discipline, and miraculous deeds. The first Arabic inscription to mention Shah Jalal, dated 1506, comes from a 'blessed building' that perhaps housed Sufis visiting his tomb, which soon became a pilgrimage site. Shah Jalal's spirit still pervades Sylhet, where some say it makes the land the richest in Bangladesh.

Ibn Batuta boated down the Meghna, in 1345, and saw "water wheels, gardens and villages such as those along the banks of the Nile in Egypt". He wrote that, "For 15 days we sailed down the river passing through villages and orchards as though we were going through a mart". He did not describe market towns, as he did routinely elsewhere. Thus, 14th century Sylhet seems to have no big market towns, but its saint from Turkestan and visitor from Morocco show it did have wide connections, and mobility changed the land in centuries to come.

Mughals brought unprecedented force. Sylhet became a Mughal frontier town on river highways to the lands of unconquered opponents, Khasis, Dimasas, Ahoms, and others. When Mughals conquered Orissa and Bengal, Afghans fled up the Meghna and became powerful around Sylhet. A Mughal fleet sailed to Sylhet, and in 1612, Mughals conquered Afghans, but highland peoples, including Khasis, Garos, Ahoms, and Dimasas, did not succumb.

Conquest invested nature with cultural politics. Afghans escaped Mughals into forested hills and haor depressions, where high caste Hindus had escaped Afghans, three centuries earlier. Myriad escape routes made most land around Sylhet impossible to conquer, until 1830, when the British finally succeeded. Until then, highbrow lowlanders considered Sylhet a wild frontier, and rulers supported settlers who would use the weight of demography to civilise the land. A seventh century inscription described Sylhet as 'outside the pale of human habitation, where there is no distinction between natural and artificial; infested by wild animals and poisonous reptiles, and covered with forest outgrowths'. Kamarupa kings gave tracts of forest to brahmans to civilise. A millennium later, Mughals gave forests to Muslims and Hindus. In the 18th century, Nawabi Faujdars and forest grants brought Sylhet firmly into the ambit of Bengali Muslim culture. Meanwhile, Rajas in Cachar and Jaintia embraced Hinduism and patronised Brahmans who expanded mixed Hindu-tribal polities and mixed tribe-and-caste societies around the Barak valley. In Cachar, Hindu rituals elevated Bodo rulers over Dimasa subjects and enabled high caste Bengalis to mix among tribal masters, neighbours, and servants, in the manner of oil on water.

Natural Economy

Over the centuries, local territories of natural resource utilisation diversified along a topographical continuum running from the highest highlands, where shifting 'jhum' cultivation prevailed, to the lowest lowlands, where farmers grew 'boro' rice, planted in December-January, when fields dry out enough to plant, and harvested before the floods arrived in May-July. In 1800, forest still covered much of the land, roughly in proportion to altitude. Permanent agriculture expanded and contracted, in fits and starts; and expansion only gained a firm upper hand in the 19th century. Farmers facing recurring flood calamities routinely abandoned old farm sites, allowing forest to return as they colonised new land. The 1780s brought the worst floods in memory, which destroyed farm investments in the years when the Tista River shifted its course, joined the Brahmaputra, and changed its course as well. The 1790s brought floods and earthquakes that demolished the lowest farmland behind the 18th century market town of Ajmiriganj, spawning endemic malaria, which stymied new colonisation until 1900.

Nature's topography defined economic geography. In the late 18th century, farming communities in the lowland floodplains grew almost nothing but 'boro' rice, which they consumed with locally abundant fish. There were no large market centres, let alone major cities, by the standards of lower Bengal, no weavers exporting cloth, and no locally resident rich merchants, let alone portfolio-capitalists. 'Hundis' were so hard to find that early Company Collectors had to ship revenues on armed boats to Dhaka. No European Company ever made a major commercial investment in the Surma basin. Yet markets thrived, as supply and demand met in countless small transactions with little input from urban commercial networks. Rulers received taxation only in cash. Specialists in fishing, horticulture, hunting, mining, trade, transportation, crafts, finance, and administration all bought rice in local lowland markets that thrived amidst the flood-induced uncertainty of local rice output. In 1790, Sylhet District had over 600 named market places (hat, ganj, and bazaar). Long-distance commodity chains passed through them, up and down the Meghna, to and from Dhaka, Narayanganj, and Bakarganj (near Barisal), and up and down the Barak valley, to and from Manipur, Assam, and Burma. As the number of market centres increased in Bengal generally, Sylhet town became a more active regional market, to which the Manipur and Tripura rajahs built a new jungle road from Manipur, in the 1790s.

Many commodities in the lowlands carried Khasi social identities. Khasi merchants brought goods from Assam through mountain river ports at Pandua and Jaintia. Khasis sold mountain 'jhum' rice in Jaintia. In high valleys and on low slopes, Khasis grew areca nut, betel, turmeric, and fruits to sell in the plains, along with wax, ivory, and cloth. Mountain Khasis also specialised in iron mining and smelting, and they would denude whole forest tracts to stoke their blow-bag iron furnaces, with cowhide bellows, before moving on to exploit new fuel wood sites. Khasi iron, steel, and metal tools travelled lowland rivers routes, along with their gold, silver, other metals, and ornaments. Khasi mountain quarries behind Sunamganj provided the finest quality limestone.

Elephants and ivory also travelled down the mountains, as salt and rice moved up. Aloe wood and China-root appear as Sylhet products in the *Ain-i-Akbari*. Timber, sandalwood, cane, ivory, rubber, cotton, and silk came from Cachar and Manipur. Cotton came from Tripura. Sylhet's first resident

Collector, Robert Lindsay, dramatised the commercial value of the mountains by buying limestone and burnt lime to sell in Dhaka, Calcutta, and elsewhere. He even once had built four sea-going ships on mountain tops, using local forest timber; and then had the ships filled with mountain products and to sail on the flood to Bakarganj, where his agents sold forest products and bought rice to sell in Madras.

These ships perhaps returned to Calcutta or Chittagong with cowry shells, Sylhet's only coin. Each part of 18th century Bengal had its own monetary identity, acquired in mobile geographies of commodity exchange. In 1787, for example, most coins in Rangpur were French Arcot Rupees, minted in Pondicherry, and Narainy Rupees, minted by rajas in Cooch Behar; while in nearby Mymensingh, English Arcot Rupees prevailed; because Rangpur did heavy trade with Cooch Behar and Chandranagore, while Mymensingh sold its rice in Calcutta. Specific coins also attached to individual commodities, as in Dinajpur, where merchants used Sonaut Rupees to buy rice and other grains, while they used French and English Arcots to buy ghee and oil, and used only French Arcots to buy hemp and gunny. Locally dominant metal coins came from far away, most of all, from Arcot and Pondicherry, and cowries came from the Maldives.

Sylhet depended entirely on cowries, tiny shells from the Maldives that served as the cheapest coin all around the Indian Ocean and in south-east Asia, and Africa. Bengal was a major cowry market, and there was virtually no metal coin to be found in Sylhet in the late 18th century, when people imported almost nothing from downstream, except the cowries that merchants brought from the Maldives, stored in Dhaka and Calcutta, and carried to Sylhet in boats that returned with rice and upland products.

The only political force at work shaping Sylhet cowry country was a negative one: that is, the weakness of regional states. English observers believed that cowries reigned in Sylhet because the people could only afford the cheapest coin. But because barter trades flourished alongside cowry exchange, it can be said that cowries also functioned to bridge the gap between barter and commerce in local markets. Cowry country had a south-western borderland, around Habiganj, where silver rupees circulated, indicating that cowry country coincided with the spatial dispersion of markets connecting hills and plains around Sylhet. The repeated depiction of Sylhet as a 'mountain region', from the 14th century onward, also reinforces the idea that mountains and lowlands comprised a diverse yet coherent economic space of mobility where cowries articulated a distinctive market territory around 18th century Sylhet.

Expansive Territorialism

In 1765, Sylhet—till then a 'faujdari' (military district) of Bengal Nawabs—became a frontier district of Bengal Presidency. Despite its large area and population, Sylhet was poor revenue territory. In 1783, the Dinajpur zamindar spent more on religious events than Sylhet district paid revenue. In 1785, the Rajshahi zamindar's monthly tax ('kist') exceeded Sylhet's annual tax assessment ('jamma'). Yet the Company increased Sylhet taxation as much as possible. The Nawab's regime had collected 3,50,000 kahans of cowries in Sylhet, all spent locally, mostly on the army, which remained the standard until 1776, when Sylhet's 'jamma' rose to 8,00,101 kahans. By 1783, it had risen to 9,36,000 kahans. State tax demands thus tripled in eight years after 1775, a much higher increase than in Bengal Presidency as a whole.

But revenue collections stagnated below 70 per cent of jamma until 1788, when they began a steep climb, approaching 100 per cent by 1790. This increase came with expansion of Company authority over farms that became tax-paying private property. In 1784, "upwards of 4,000 independent proprietors of the soil" paid land taxes; in 1795, 26,000; and in 1798, 27,000. In 1785. remittances to Calcutta began a steady climb, and in the 1790s, with the addition of the region around Habiganj, Sylhet district began to look like a money-maker for the Raj, though a small one compared to other Bengal districts.

In Sylhet (as in Chittagong), Company revenue came from small village landlords, not big zamindars, merchant magnates, or big 'jotedar' tenants who dominate the agrarian history of Bengal. Even the smallest Sylheti landowners rarely tilled their land, but rather employed tenants and labourers. To secure assets against calamity, locally dominant families held land in several places and combined various sources of income, including commerce, which made them central figures in local markets and revenue operations. For tenants and labourers, mobility remained an always-open option. Most tenants were 'paikasht' or non-resident tenants, who received no occupancy rights but did receive agricultural and subsistence inputs from landowners who needed to attract them to clear and cultivate land. Landless workers also lived mobile lives. Some would have come from tribal societies that moved among hills and plains and merged with lowland societies at the lowest ranks. Seasonal migrant workers often came from far away to bring in the harvest and return home with boatloads of rice.

In 1798, a statistically average Sylhet village would have held a tiny population of about 70 people and four landed estates ('taluks'), each estate representing one extended family, it dependents and servants. Local farming territory expanded in compact areas scattered across the land, as dominant families spread their influence and vied for land and labour. Many such families held the title of Chaudhuri, which Mughals used to denote sub-zamindari authority and which spread among Sylhet gentry to become a family name. Mughal governors anointed few if any major zamindars, one of whom an early Collector called the 'only true zamindar' in the Sylhet District, because he had received a Mughal jaghir for protecting Mughal territory against Khasi incursions.

Unconquered Mughal opponents still exercised power in Sylhet in the early Company decades. Khasis ruled the northern mountains, Jaintia Khasi rajas held land in the north and east, Cachar rajas held the Barak Valley, and Tripura rajas ruled southern uplands. The Mughals had kept them all at bay with arms and land grants, but the main source of Mughal strength locally seems to have been several thousand local landed patriarchs who acquired the title of Chaudhuri as they bowed to the Mughals.

By 1778, when the first English Collector arrived and the District Records begin, the titular name, Chaudhuri, was a purely local asset in Sylhet, where local patriarchs expanded their reach as rulers in the hills also extended their powers in the plains. Like Mughals and Nawabs, the English lacked power in the mountains and focused their attention on the lowlands, from which they eventually extended lowland power farther into uplands than any predecessor. Here as elsewhere in British India, the 19th century conquest of mountains by lowland territorialism became a topographical signature of modernity.

The Company's early steps set the modern trajectory, by separating Company lowlands from the highlands. Collectors settled borders with Cachar, Jaintia, Tripura by transacting with established Rajas, who had long experience with lowland rulers. Khasis in northern mountains posed a more difficult problem, because they had never submitted to Mughal or Nawabi authority and their people still scattered across the land north of the Surma, while some distant relatives—frontier settlers below the mountains, called Bengali Khasis—emerged from alliances between Khasis and Bengalis and defied the authority of Company and Khasi rulers alike.

Agrarian lowlanders and Khasi peoples conceived territorialism quite differently. For the Company, as for the Mughals, territory was land; but for Khasis, territory was Khasi people. As the English sought to fix boundaries of state territory, Khasi territory moved and scattered with Khasi settlements. Khasi rulers in the hills presumed authority over Khasi communities living in territory where the Company claimed exclusive authority over all the land and inhabitants. These conflicting visions of territory produced serious conflict in the 1780s.

In 1789, following many skirmishes, mountain Khasis and Bengali Khasis attacked Company settlements, and the Collector summoned troops to push Khasis into the hills. This accomplished, in 1790, he declared an absolute boundary at the base of the hills and prohibited Khasis from owning land in the plains, to vitiate future claims by Khasi rulers to Company land. Hill trades hence came under strict regulation. A modern border came into being, which would eventually separate Indian Meghalaya from Bangladeshi Sylhet.

Khasi hills thus acquired an official ethnic identity, as hill Khasis became official aliens in the plains. By 1797, Bengali farmers paying Company revenue had colonised land formerly held by Bengali Khasis, whose land the Company expropriated and who faded from history with the separation of Bengali and Khasi ethnic territories. This same border also confirmed Khasi authority, however, in what eventually became Meghalaya, as Cachar, Jaintia, and Tripura remained open frontiers for lowland settlers, who swarmed into the frontiers after 1800, while few lowlanders ever settled in Khasi mountains.

In the 19th century, Sylhet territorialism also moved into its southern mountain frontiers, behind Maulvi Bazar and Habiganj, where English-owned tea estates took the land of forest peoples. These mountains and their inhabitants fanned out into plains east of the Meghna, and extended across Tripura, Manipur, Chittagong and Burma. Mountain societies remained mobile, as their land fell to the steady influx of lowland colonisers. Ethnic conflict over land ensued, along with complex cultural mixing and tense ambiguities of political authority. Like Khasis in the north, Tripuri people in the south continued to live, settle, work, and move across the uplands and lowlands, as they became official aliens in the plains; but unlike the Meghalaya mountains, Tripura frontiers in southern Sylhet remained open for lowland territorial expansion, like Cachar and Jaintia.

The uphill march of lowland territorialism accelerated after 1800, 1880 and 1947. More and more Hindus, Muslims, and Christians made mountains their private property. Hill peoples became minorities in the hills. After 1947, mobility among peoples variously invested in mountain resources fell into but also a foul of territorial strictures imposed by national states. As a result, we have, on the one hand, this placid imagery from the 'Visit Bangladesh' website:

Nestled in the picturesque Surma Valley amidst scenic tea plantations and lush green tropical forests, Sylhet is a prime attraction for all tourists visiting Bangladesh. Lying between the Khasia and the Jaintia hills on the north, and the Tripura hills on the south, Sylhet breaks the monotony of the flatness of this land by a multitude of terraced tea gardens, rolling countryside and exotic flora and fauna. Here the thick tropical forests abound with many species of wild life, scented orange groves and luxuriant pineapple plantations spread their aroma around the typical hearth and homes of the Manipuri Tribal maidens famous for their dance.

And on the other hand, we have news about violence. On August 5, 2002, the *Daily Star* reported that Bangladesh forest department officials and 'bands of local miscreants' had forcefully evicted from forests in Moulvibazar Zila 20 of 1,000 Khasi families growing betel there for generations. This one eviction drive (among many) had killed one person and injured several others, as part of an effort to create an eco-park as a tourist attraction. On February 2, 2002, *Frontline* reported much worse violence on the Indian side of the border:

Ethnic violence in Tripura and Assam claimed 56 lives with a span of 10 days in mid-January. The victims were Bengalis and Hindi-speaking Biharis and the killers were tribal extremists belonging to the National Liberation Front of Tripura (NLFT) and the National Democratic Front of Bodoland (NDFB). The tribal militants in Tripura, who belong to either the NLFT or the All Tripura Tiger Force (ATTF), have persistently followed a policy of ethnic cleansing. They want Bengalis to move out of the state where the tribal people once formed the majority community. Militant tribal leaders know that they cannot achieve this objective, as Bengalis now constitute over 60 per cent of the state's population... Extremists in Tripura enjoy an operational advantage as the State is surrounded on three sides by Bangladesh. They have their hideouts in Bangladesh where they find easy shelter when under pressure from the security forces.

Sylheti Territory

Human mobility changed the cultural mix of societies in the region as Sylhet district moved—four times—among state jurisdictions. During a century in Bengal Presidency (1765-

1874), Sylhet inhabited moving frontiers of British imperialism, which spread to borders of Burma and China and, for the first time, surrounded Sylhet with state boundaries on all sides. In this context, a mixed flow of immigrants arrived, including tea plantation workers, whose English employers captured Sylhet's southern hills and led Sylhet district into an Assam 'Planters' Raj'. In 1871, people classified as Hindu and Muslim in the census each comprised half the district population, and brahmans were 6 per cent of Hindus, more than in most predominantly Hindu regions of British India. In 1900, Sylhet's cultural mix included a Sylheti literary movement, led by Moulvi Abdul Karim, who printed books in his Siloti Nagri font, at his Islamia Press, and flourishing traditions of Sanskrit scholarship.

The Muslim population apparently began its proportionate rise after 1808, when an estimate of a 2:3 ratio of Muslims to Hindus implies a Muslim increase by one-third in the next six decades, to generate a 1:1 ratio in 1871. After the move to Assam, the proportion of Muslims rose in each census. Immigration was clearly the cause. In 1911, people reportedly born in Mymensingh composed per cent of the population of the Assam valley (including Sylhet), and they numbered 63 per cent in 1931. This mobility then acquired new territorial meaning. In 1931, the Assam Census Report called Muslim Bengalis 'invaders' and the Assam Congress resolved to move Sylhet out of Assam. The Partition Plan produced a Sylhet referendum, after which, a truncated Sylhet district entered East Pakistan, as the region acquired its current perimeter. After Partition, immigration radically transformed Sylhet: in the decade after 1961, the population grew 37 per cent; and in the decade after 1971, it grew 22 per cent. A hundred thousand Muslim Bengalis moved out of Assam into Sylhet's haor basin, where land still lay open for colonisation. In 1951, the proportion of Muslims reached 68 per cent, and then rose faster.

The Sylhet region today has a distinct territorial identity, and 'Sylheti' merits designation as a regional ethnicity in Bangladesh. Historically, Sylheti identity includes a long association with Assam. Sylheti language differs markedly from standard Bengali. The Sylheti literary movement that began in 1860 has been revived in recent decades. Socially, Sylhetis seem 'clannish', the word I hear most often when Sylhetis in Dhaka describe their marriage strategies and business networks. Sylhetis have a reputation for conservative gender relations, manifest publicly by pardah, as in haor communities, where Muslim women from other districts work in agriculture, but Sylhetis do not. Shah Jalal represents a spiritual centre for regional piety in Sylhet, where people identify most intensely with his legacy.

Sylheti identity is also invested in nature. Alongside the Bangladeshi nationality of nature in Bangladesh, we find a Sylheti identity of nature in Sylhet. Tourist advertisements, like the one above, represent a unique Sylhet landscape, where plans for an eco park on a national forest land brought the expulsion of Khasi residents, and where the exotic image of 'Manipuri maidens' mingles with the smell of pineapple plantations. In Sylhet, international conflicts on the border with Meghalaya have a definite local flavour, harking back to 1791.

Local Territory

In 19th century Sylhet, local landed families held local authority. Recording, adjudicating, and protecting private property rights became the main function of government. Government never meddled in local estates. The Rent Act of 1859 had no impact. When Sylhet moved into Assam, it escaped later Bengal tenancy reforms. Local Sylhet territorialism became a constituent of modern governance and of Sylhet regional identity, which however distinctive, reflects a broader pattern, because all across the land that became Bangladesh, British authority attached itself to the local gentry. Trends after 1947 nationalised this pattern. In 1951, Zamindari Abolition in east Pakistan multiplied private property rights and produced new forms of tenancy." At the same time, the 1945 Famine Inquiry Commission's conclusion that requisitioning rice for public distribution lay beyond the state's capacity in Bengal proved prophetic," when Pakistan state requisitions pnluced intense local opposition, stoked violence against Hindu traders, and helped to kill the Muslim League in east Pakistan, in the 1954 elections. In the Pakistan context, Bengali visions of Bangladesh developed inside local traditions of local authority.

Sylhetis nonetheless constitute locality in their own distinctive cultural terms, as a place of belonging; and also, in standard political and economic terms, as a spatial domain for local investments. Being well placed in local society provides key people with privileged access to networks of connectivity that expand their opportunities in wider worlds of mobility. In Sylhet, intersections of mobility and territorialism assume a distinctive regional form inside social spaces composed of Sylheti 'gushti' (patrilineages).

These intersections appear in various geographical domains, where territorialism meets mobility. One is the Haor Basin. A haor is a deep radial depression that fills up to the brim and often overflows with the monsoon, and dry up sufficiently for boro rice cultivation between January and May. Farming communities occupy natural ridges and built-up land around the lakes, lapped by deep waters that cover haors from June to December. There are countless haors in Sylhet, but the western Haor Basin is entirely covered with haors and deeply flooded annually by meandering branches of the Surma and Kushiara. In this area, investments in agriculture have been hard to secure and large tracts remained open for new colonisation as late as 1950.

Compact enclaves ('bari') of related families ('gushti') form settlements on haor lands, where local Sylheti landlords held sway, before 1950, and locals reproduced landlordism thereafter, as the land filled up with immigrant settlers. Communities establish residential sites based on their common place of origin, occupational and religious groups also formed mini-territories on haor ridges. As in most of agrarian south Asia, micro-ethnic partitions of local agrarian territory occurred as the region attained an overarching ethnic identity defined by the cultural affinities of the major landowning groups. Today, the regional identity is Bengali Muslim, in the frame of Bangladesh, and Sylheti, in the frame of Sylhet.

Topography articulates inequality among families on haor land. Higher, wider ridges are wealthier and more populous.

Lower lands that extend across deeper, wider hoar lakes host more precarious, poorer communities, filled with seasonal migrants who still come to harvest boro crops. On the widest, richest hoar ridges, wealthier families live on higher land, less vulnerable to flooding. Upwardly mobile families buy higher, more profitable farmland, just below the hoar ridge; and they live in higher, drier residential sites, atop the ridge. Poorer and downwardly mobile families can buy more land at lower prices for housing at the lowest edge of ridge, nearest the lake, where their homes feel the lapping of floods; and they can also buy farmland more cheaply farther out in the haor lakes, where floods come sooner, lands produce less, and work is harder and less profitable.

We find a different but also typically Sylheti intersection of mobility and territorialism in and around the towns of Sylhet, Sunamganj, Moulvibazar, and Habibganj, which provide sites for local investments by Sylheti families most visibly marked big, fancy, brightly painted houses. These houses belong to families in *gushti* whose men went to London, generations ago—some as early as the late 18th century—originally as workers on ships, who eventually opened restaurants. British immigration laws of the 20th century restricted Sylheti immigration to the relatives of earlier Sylheti settlers in London, and fostered a Sylheti monopoly of the London 'Indian restaurant' business. Today, Sylheti Londoni families have created a mobile territory of business activity, anchored in Sylhet and London, composed of Bangladesh and UK citizens.' In recent decades, these transnational locals have been most active in organisations devoted to making Sylheti language, literature, and regional identity more publicly visible.

Like others who have built family business domains in south Asia, Londoni Sylhetis invest meticulously in marriage, religion, and other social activities to enhance their family status, cultural capital, and business assets (which include dependable partners, financiers, and employees). Young Sylheti women, born and raised in London, travel to their family's home village in Sylhet to marry selected men from appropriate families. When immigration officials allow, the husband joins his wife in London to work in his father-in-law's restaurant, while his wife, typically more educated and always more westernised, follows other suitable occupations. In time, sons-in-law can attain UK citizenship and thus the basis for a break with the family, but the independence of Londoni brides can cause more difficult problems. Should daughters marry men not of their parents' choice in Sylhet, family struggles might ensue in which parents seek redress for the loss of honour and prospects, and as UK citizens, dissident Londoni brides can enlist the help of the British High Commission in Dhaka to return independently to England.

Londoni families seem to address their family legal dilemmas mostly by using local police and state courts, but less well-endowed Sylhetis often resort to informal mediation hearings, called 'shalish', a distinctive local institution in Bangladesh. Conflicts over land and other property preoccupy about half of all 'shalish' mediations, where local men of authority, convened ad hoc and case-by-case, sit to hear the troubles and make a judgment. Its informality makes the shalish difficult to historicise, but a new historical phase clearly began in 1993, when one Sylheti shalish issued a fatwa to punish a woman and her father for her 'illicit' marital union, by caning him and stoning her, after which, she committed suicide. Similar events elsewhere have spurred public campaigns to reform the local shalish in conformity with Bangladesh national law.

Conclusion

Investments in nature in Sylhet operate in local, regional, and national territories that mobility has been reshaping for a very long time. Mobility is still reshaping Bangladesh. Activists, researchers, and officials travel the country to bring localities into the national project of development. Packed planes fly to and from London and Sylhet. Villagers flock to cities and to Persian Gulf economies that send funds back to support Islamic endeavours. International capital and commodity flows sustain a Bangladesh readymade garments industry to benefit consumers in America. The US government tries to force Bangladesh to export natural gas from Sylhet to India, to profit the US oil companies. Goods and people move massively across international borders. The Indian government decries Bangladeshi 'infiltrators'. The Indian military pushes Bengali Muslims into Bangladesh. Tripura rebels find refuge in mobile spaces that defy national maps.

Ideas and information that we use typically to comprehend such transactions between mobility and territorialism etch the black-and-white lines of national geography. History in Sylhet indicates a rather more complex, diverse spatial reality, composed of many grey areas and shifting, overlapping social spaces. By exploring the grey areas of history, we can better analyse modern structural transformations and discontinuities, which take shape at shifting intersections of mobility and territorialism.

The practical lesson is this: the mobility that characterises globalisation today operates simultaneously in many spatial and temporal registers, and forms many geographies, which coexist, conflict, and complicate one another, and have done for a very long time. In the modern world of capitalism, where investments move to places that provide the best returns, and dividends move into the hands of people 'in the loop' of capital accumulation; the biggest winners are the richest folks in rich countries and rich urban neighbourhoods; but local families constitute 'the loop' in countless localities, where the mobility of people, assets, and state power intersect in territories of capital accumulation. National politicians and intellectuals who work in shifting spatial domains that span local and global geographies would thus do well to abandon the idea that static national maps represent the basic facts of modern geography.

6

Politics and Economics of Oil

The annals of oil are an uninterrupted chronicle of naked aggression, genocide and the violent law of the corporate frontier. Iraq was born from this vile trinity. In their own way, the awful spectacle of oil-men parading through the corridors of the White House, the rise of militant Islamism across the Quran belt, and the carnage on the road to Baghdad, all bear out the dreadful dialectics of blood and oil. Paul Wolfowitz's recent confession, to the Asian Security Summit in Singapore in early June, that the Iraq war driven not by the fiction of weapons of mass destruction but by the 'simple fact' that the 'country swims on a sea of oil' is consistent at least with the last eighty years of US foreign policy [Painter 1986]. But there is another oil story in train, bearing all the hallmarks of the long, ugly history petrolic violence. Two years ago, vice president Dick Cheney predicted that Africa would become the fastest growing source of oil for the American market (as much as 25 per cent of US imports by 2015) and it is hardly a surprise to learn there where oil reigns supreme the military are sure to follow. *The Wall Street Journal* reported several weeks ago that the Pentagon, in the most radical deployment of American forces since the end of the cold war, will move troops from Germany to the Caucasus and west Africa to 'protect key oil reserves'. More oil, more blood.

Protection demands, of course, keeping the oil flowing by working hand-in-hand with a phalanx of African dictators and political psychopaths on the one side, and super majors like Exxon-Mobil and Chevron-Texaco on the other who, citing confidentiality agreements, refuse to disclose the fees, royalties and other services (paramilitaries and security forces among them) made to the phalanxes of well-placed African nomenclature. Such is the scale of the decrepitude and venality—$ 300 million in Equatorial Guinea, billions in Nigeria over the last two decades—that Tony Blair is now in a trans-Atlantic tug of war to have oil majors disclose their payments for leases and concessions, a proposal fiercely resisted by American big oil and the Bush administration. In a separate proposal George Soros calls for mandatory reporting as a prerequisite for listing of oil companies on the world's stock exchanges. In the last year a raft of new reports inventory the appalling record of oil-based economies in relation to corruption, economic growth and poverty alleviation. Oil, as Anderson says, is thicker than blood or water.

Another Oil Story

A year before the events of September 11, 2001, the US department of state in its annual encyclopaedia of 'global terrorism' identified the Niger delta—the ground zero of oil production in Nigeria—as a breeding ground for increasingly militant 'impoverished ethnic groups' for whom terrorist acts (abduction, hostage taking, kidnapping and extra-judicial killings) against foreigners were legion. The CIA concurred (2000), laying emphasis on the catalytic effects of 'environmental stresses' in the oil-rich southern delta on 'political tensions'. At this time, Nigeria—the 13th largest producer of petroleum (and which provides 80 per cent of government revenues, 95 per cent of export receipts, and 90 per cent of foreign exchange earnings)—was providing almost 14 per cent of US American petroleum consumption. At about the same time, the Petroleum Finance Company (PFC) presented to the US congressional international relations committee sub-committee on Africa a report of the strategic and growing security significance of west African oil whose high quality reserves and low cost output—coupled with massive new deep-water discoveries—required, in the view of PFC, serious attention, and substantial foreign investment. In the wake of the Al Qaeda attacks, and on the larger canvas of the crisis in Venezuela and the Iraq war, west Africa has emerged as the site of 'the new Gulf oil states'. Indeed by January 2002 the Institute for Advanced Strategic and Political Studies was providing a forum for the Bush oil-administration to declare that African oil is 'a priority for US national security'. In the last year, Africa's black gold-in Gabon, SaoTome, Angola, Equatorial Guinea—and its ugly footprint are rarely off the front pages. Oil and blood, as Jon Anderson put it, are ubiquitous. With the additional frisson of terrorism: the 'nightmare', as the New York Times noted, of 'sympathisers of Osama bin Laden sink(ing) three oil tankers in the straits of Hormuz'.

The myths of oil and oil-wealth has been central to the history of modern industrial capitalism. But in Nigeria, as elsewhere in, the discovery of oil, and annual oil revenues of $ 40 billion currently, has ushered in a miserable, undisciplined, decrepit, and corrupt form of 'petro-capitalism'. After a half century of oil production from which almost $ 300 billion in oil revenues have flowed directly into the federal exchequer (and perhaps 50 billion promptly flowed out only to 'disappear' overseas), Nigerian per capita income stands at $ 290 per year. For the majority of Nigerians, living standards are no better now than at independence in 1960. A repugnant culture of excessive venality and profiteering among the political class—the department of state has an entire website devoted to so-called 419 fraud cases—confers upon Nigeria the dubious honour of sitting step Transparency International's ranking of most corrupt states. Paradoxically, oil-producing states in the federation—the Niger delta—have benefited the least from oil-wealth. Devastated by the ecological costs of oil spillage and the highest gas flaring rates in the world, the Niger delta is a political tinderbox. A generation of militant 'restive' youth, deep political frustrations among oil-producing communities, and pre-electoral thuggery all combine to prosper in the rich soil of political marginalisation. The massive rigging of elections across the delta in the April 2003 elections simply confirmed the worst for the millions of Nigerians who have suffered from decades of neglect.

The middle-east historian Robert Vitalis (2001) has recently suggested that the rapid, complete and irreversible rise of American dominance in Saudi Arabia can shed much light on why 'the Niger delta is currently in crisis'. And indeed it is. Since March 12, 2003, mounting communal violence accounting for at least 50 deaths, and the levelling of eight communities in and around the Warri petroleum complex, has prompted all the major oil companies to withdraw staff, to close down operations and reduce output by over 7,50,000 barrels per day (almost half of national output). President Obasanjo has dispatched large troop deployments to the oil-producing creeks, prompting Ijaw militants, incensed over indiscriminate military action and illegal oil bunkering in which the security forces were implicated, to threaten the detonation of eleven captured oil installations. The strikes on the off-shore oil platforms—a long-festering sore that rarely reaches the media—were quickly resolved but nobody seriously expects that the deeper problems within the oil sector will go away. Relatively new to delta politics, however, are a series of assassinations, the most shocking being the killing of chief Marshall Harry, a senior member of the main opposition party and leading campaigner for greater resource allocation to the oil-producing Niger delta. Fallout from the Harry assassination has already become a source of tension in his native oil-producing state of rivers where supporters of the main opposition party, the ANPP and another opposition grouping of activists and politicians, the Rivers Democratic Movement, have linked the ruling party to the assassination. With good reason, the business-as-usual character of the gubernatorial election victories across the oil-producing states, has led some to believe that the Nigeria is another Colombia in the making [Cesarz et al 2003].

The strategic significance of Nigeria is incontestable. One of every five Africans is a Nigerian, Nigeria is the world's seventh largest exporter of petroleum and a key player in African regional security, most recently in Sierra Leone. Nigeria is an archetypal oil nation. Three quarters of government revenues, and almost all export earnings, flow from black gold. A long-time member of OPEC, and the fifth largest supplier of oil exports to the US, Nigeria pumps oil much coveted for its 'lightness' and 'sweetness', yielding more gasoline and diesel than the 'sour' crude from the Middle East. It is also home to a vast Muslim community. Since the oil boom of the 1970s, political power has shifted from the conservative Sufi brotherhoods to well-organised modern Islamist groups like the Yan Izala founded in 1978. Sharia'a law, of a dogmatic and literalist sort, has been adopted and implemented in 12 of the populous northern states, amidst considerable political acrimony and international censure. At least 350 people were killed in four days of terrible rioting in northern Nigeria triggered by protests against US military action in Afghanistan, including particularly bloody clashes between Muslims and Christians in Kano, Kaduna and Jos.

Olesegun Obasanjo's presidential victory in 1999, in the wake of the darkest period of military rule in Nigeria's 40 year post-independence history, held much promise. An internationally recognised statesman and diplomat imprisoned during the brutal Abacha years, he inherited the mantle of a massively corrupt state apparatus, an economy in shambles, and a federation crippled by long-standing ethnic enmity. Committed to reforming a corrupt and undisciplined military—the largest in Africa—and to deepening the process of democratisation, Obasanjo was confronted within months of his inauguration by militant ethnic groups speaking the language of self-determination, local autonomy and resource control (meaning a greater share of the federally allocated oil revenues). In an incident widely condemned by the human rights community, some 2,000 persons were slaughtered in Odi, Bayelsa state after federal troops were dispatched in response to clashes between local militants and the police. Obasanjo has consistently refused to apologise for the murders and there has been no full inquiry. Last year the military was involved in yet another massacre, this time in the middle-belt, in Benue and Taraba states, the most serious communal conflict since the clashes preceding the outbreak of the Biafran civil war in 1967. On president Obasanjo's watch, over 10,000 have perished in ethnic violence. He has failed miserably to address the human rights violations by the notoriously corrupt Nigerian security forces. Early in his tenure, Obasanjo did retire a number of senior officers and embark upon an anti-corruption campaign, aided and abetted by the US's role in 'retraining' the Nigerian armed forces. President Clinton committed foreign assistance to 'reprofessionalise' the Nigerian army in 1999, including the equipping and training of seven battalions at a cost of over $1 billion. During the Bush imperium, the presence of 200 special forces in Nigeria, including on-site training grounds in some of the most sensitive areas of the Muslim north, has generated enormous suspicion and now vocal opposition. Not unexpectedly, a number of powerful Nigerian constituencies see a beleaguered and corrupt Obasanjo regime as simply another miserable US oil colony.

The Zeitgeist of oil—its mythic and spectacular qualities in relation to the modern—is an essential expression of contemporary hydro-carbon capitalism. Oil's fetishistic appeal was not lost on the great Polish journalist Ryszard Kapucinksi who, in his reflections on oil-rich pre-revolutionary Iran, sardonically observed that, "Oil creates the illusion of a completely changed life, life without work, life for free....The concept of oil expresses perfectly the eternal human dream of wealth achieved through lucky accident...In this sense oil is a fairy tale and like every fairy tale a bit of a lie" (1982: 35). It is this lie, one might say, that currently confronts west African oil producers, and Nigeria in particular.

A Resource Curse?

In virtue of the geo-strategic significance of oil to contemporary capitalism—and to US hegemony in particular—relations between natural resources (and oil in particular) and economic growth, democracy, and civil war have emerged as an object of substantial scholarly attention (operating under the sign of 'resource polities'), not least by economists and political scientists.

The IMF and its stenographers have posited a strong association between resource-dependency, corruption and economic performance. Sachs and Warner (1995) argue that one standard deviation increase in the ratio of natural resource exports to GNP is associated with a decrease of just over 1 per cent in the growth rate (irrespective of the endogeneity of corruption, commodity price variability and trade liberalisation). Leite and Weidemann (1999) believe that for fuels the figure is 0.6 per cent and due 'entirely to the indirect effect of corruption' (1999:29). For Michael Klare (2001), writing from a very different vantage point, oil is a dwindling, key-strategic resource that will necessarily be generative of interstate conflict (see also Homer-Dixon 1999).'2 This is a line of argumentation developed by Paul Collier, who, in his work with the World Bank, uses resource dependency as a way of thinking about rebellion (especially in Africa), with oil posited as central to the economics of civil war. It encourages extortion and looting through resource predation (at least up to the point where 26 per cent of GDP is dependent on resource extraction). And the feasibility of predation by states or rebel groups determines the risk of conflict. For Collier, the risks are greater because of resource dependency than ethnic or religious diversity. Oil is a 'resource curse'. Ross elaborates on this claim seeing oil in terms of its rentier effect (low taxes and high patronage dampen pressures for democracy); its repression effect conferred by the direct state control over sufficient revenues to bankroll excessive military expenditures and expanded internal security apparatuses; and a modernisation effect, namely, the 'move into industrial and service sector jobs render them less likely to push for democracy' (2001:357). This comes terribly close to a sort of commodity determinism confirming perhaps Coronil's point that oil, more than any other commodity, 'illustrates both the importance and the mystification of natural resources in the modern world' [Coronil 1997: 49]. But if oil hinders democracy (as though copper might liberate parliamentary democracy?), one needs to appreciate the centralising effect of oil and the state in relation to the oil-based nation-building enterprises that are unleashed in the context of a politics that predates oil.

Much of the resource curse analysis runs the risk of imputing enormous powers to oil (without grasping its specificity), conflating petroleum's purported Olympian powers with preexisting political dynamics, and, as in the case of Collier, misidentifying a predation-proneness for what is in fact the dynamics of state and corporate enclave politics [Leonard and Strauss 2003]. What is striking in so much of what passes as 'resource polities' is the total invisibility of both transnational oil companies (which typically work in joint ventures with the state) and the specific forms of rule associated with petro-capitalism. My analysis charts the relations between oil and violence, but does so through examining how forms of governable (or non-governable spaces) are created through the analytics of 'authoritarian governmentality' [Dean 1999] growing out of the soil of petro-capitalism. Rather than see oil-dependency as a source of predation or as a source of state military power, I explore how oil capitalism produces particular sorts of enclave economies and particular sorts of governable spaces characterised by violence and instability. To do so, the qualities of oil in relation to predation matter (oil and diamonds are after all very different sources of predation: see Le Billon 2001). But so do the powers of transnational oil companies, the character of what I call 'the oil complex', and the ways in which oil as a territorially-based and nationalised commodity can become the basis for making claims. Unlike the work of Collier and others, I seek to trace the varieties of violence engendered by oil, to elaborate the ways in which resources, territoriality and identity can constitute forms of rule (or unrule), and understand the genesis of economies of violence that emerge from differing sorts of governable (or ungovernable) spaces.

Black Gold and Niger Delta

The Niger delta is a vast sedimentary basin constructed through successive layers of sediments dating back 40-50 million years to the Eocene epoch. A classic arcuate delta covering almost 70,000 square kilometres, the Niger delta is also endowed with very substantial hydrocarbon deposits. Crude oil production currently runs at almost two million barrels per day, roughly 90 per cent by value of Nigerian export revenues. Nigeria is not only the largest producer of petroleum in Africa and is among the world's top 10 oil producers but, in the wake of September 11 and the current west Asia crisis, it is being pursued by the Bush administration as a major supplier for the US market.

The contemporary geo-strategic significance of the Niger delta has emerged from an astonishing ethnic and linguistic complexity, and from a recent history of economic and political irrelevance. There are five major linguistic categories (Ijoid, Yoruboid, Edoid, Igboid and Delta Cross), but each embraces a profusion of ethno-linguistic heterogeneity. The establishment of the Nigerian colony and the imposition of indirect rule in the early 1900s marked an end to the brief period of commercial vitality associated with the commercialisation of palm oil across the region in the 19th century. For most of the first half of the 20th century, the delta was an economic and political backwater. In the gradual transition to independence in the 1950s, the so-called ethnic minorities voiced their concerns to the departing British administrators that their interests in a Nigerian federation dominated by three ethnic majorities (the Hausa, the Yoruba and the Ibo) were to all intents and purposes invisible. What was true at the moment of imperial departure only became more so as the post-colonial period got under way.

The onset of commercial petroleum production in the heart of the delta in 1956—discovered in Oloibiri in current Bayelsa state—seemed to hold out the promise of rapid development for the ethnic minorities. But instead, the presence of transnational oil companies in joint ventures with the Nigerian state (through the Nigerian National Petroleum Company (NNPC)) produced enormous environmental despoliation and a crisis in extant forms of livelihood. By the 1970s and 1980s, a number of ethnic communities had begun to mobilise against the so-called 'slick alliance' of oil companies and the Nigerian military. Most famously, the movement for the survival of the Ogoni People (MOSOP) led by Ken Saro-Wiwa challenged Shell for its environmental despoliation and human rights violations and the Nigerian state for its unjust control of 'their oil'. Saro-Wiwa and the MOSOP leadership were executed by the Nigerian military in 1995, but since that time the Niger delta has become a zone of intense conflict as more oil-producing minorities (for instance, the Adoni, the Itsekiri, the Ijaw) clamour for compensation and for the recognition of their claims for resource control. As I write, substantial coverage in the world press has been devoted to a group of delta women who have occupied Chevron oil refineries, demanding company investments and jobs for indigenes.

I want to make three important points about oil in Nigeria. The first is that oil capitalism operates through what I call an 'oil complex' (comparable in, say, Venezuela or Gabon or Indonesia) involving a statutory monopoly over mineral exploitation (the 1969 Petroleum Law in Nigeria, reinforced by a number of key laws including the 1978 Land Use Decree), a nationalised oil company (NNPC) that operates through joint ventures with oil majors who are granted territorial concessions (blocs), the security apparatuses of the state (and the companies) to ensure that costly investments are secured, the oil producing communities, and apolitical mechanism (in Nigeria called the 'derivation principle') by which federal oil revenues are distributed to the states [Ibeanu 2003, Anugwom 2001]. This oil complex—rather than a laundry list of oil-attributes a la Ross, is key to understanding the relations between oil and violence. The second is that this oil complex matters profoundly to the character and dynamics of Nigerian development. Oil is, of course, a biophysical entity (a subterranean fluid capable of being pumped and transmitted); it is also a commodity that enters the market with its price tag, and as such is the bearer of particular relations of production. And, not least, oil harbours fetishistic qualities: it is the bearer of meanings, hopes, expectations of unimaginable powers. Not unexpectedly, oil is a constant in the popular Nigerian imagination [Watts 2000], resplendent with all manner of brilliant and unctuous qualities. The third point is that Nigerian petro-capitalisrn contained a sort of double-movement, a contradictory unity of capitalism and modernity captured in the fact that oil production in Nigeria has always been a joint venture, currently with 14 transnational companies, in which joint operating agreements determine the distribution of royalties and rents. On the one hand, oil has been a centralising force that has rendered the state more visible and globalised, underwriting a process of secular nationalism and state building. On the other, a corrupt and undisciplined oil-led development, driven by an unremitting political logic of ethnic claims-making, has fragmented and discredited the state and its forms of governance. It has produced a set of conditions that have compromised and undermined the very tenets of the modern nation state. Coronil (1997) refers to this conundrum as 'the Faustian trade of money for modernity', which in Venezuela brought 'the illusion of development'. In Nigeria, too, the double movement brought illusion and produced forms of governable spaces that questioned the very idea of Nigeria, spaces that generated forms of rule, conduct and imagining at cross purposes with one another, antithetical to the very idea of a coherent modern nation state that oil, in the myths of the west, represented.

Economies of Violence and Governable Spaces

Government, for Michel Foucault (2000), referred famously to the 'conduct of conduct', a more or less calculated and rational set of ways of shaping conduct and securing rule through a multiplicity of authorities and agencies in and outside the state and at a variety of spatial levels. In contrast to forms of pastoral power in the middle ages from which a sense of sovereignty was derived, Foucault charted an important historical shift, beginning in the 16th century, toward government as a right manner of disposing things 'so as to not lead to the common good...but to an end that is convenient for each of the things governed' (2000: 211). The new practices of the state, as Mitchell Dean (1999:16) says, shape human conduct by 'working through our desire, aspirations, interests and beliefs for definite but shifting ends'. It was Foucault's task to reveal the genealogy of government, and the origins and modern power, the fabrication of a modern identity. The conduct of conduct—governmentality—could be expressed as pastoral, disciplinary or as biopower. Modern governmentality was rendered distinctive by the specific forms in which the population and the economy were administered, and specifically by a deepening of the 'governmentalisation of the. state' (how sovereignty comes to be articulated through the populations and the processes that constitute them). What was key for Foucault was not the displacement of one form of power by another, nor the historical substitution of feudal by modern governmentality, but the complex triangulation involved in sustaining many forms of power put to the purpose of security and regulation [Foucault 2000: 219].

On this theoretical canvas, I seek to explore the relations between two interrelated aspects of governmentality. One is what Foucault explicitly refers to as relations between men and resources (in my case, people and oil in the Niger delta) as an expression of his complex notion of the governance of things. As he put it:

> On the contrary, in [the modern exercise of power], you will notice that the definition of government in no way refers to territory: one governs things. But what does this mean? I think this is not a matter of opposing things to men, but rather of showing that what government has to do with is not territory but, rather, a sort of complex composed on men and things. The things, in this sense, with which government is to be concerned are in fact men, but men in their relations, their links, their imbrication with those things that are wealth, resources, means of subsistence, the territory with its specific qualities, climate, irrigation, fertility, and so on; men in their relation to those other things that are customs, habits, ways of acting and thinking and so on; and finally men in relation to those still other things that might be accidents and misfortunes such as famines, epidemics, death and so on...What counts is essentially this complex of men and things; property and territory are merely one of its variables (2000: 208-209)

The other aspect of governmentality that I use is taken from Rose's notion of 'governable spaces' as they emerge from the analytics of government detailed above. For Rose, governable spaces and the spatialisation of government, are 'modalities in which a real and material governable world is composed, terraformed, and populated' (1999: 32). The scales upon which government is 'territorialised'—territory is derived from terra, land, but also terrere, to frighten—are myriad: the factory, the neighbourhood, the commune, the region, the nation. Each of these governable spaces has its own topology and is modelled, as Rose puts it—through systems of cognition and remodelled through government practice—in a way that frames how such topoi have emerged: the social thought and practice that has territorialised itself upon the nation, the city, the village or the factory. The map has been central to this process as a mode of objectification, marking and inscribing but also as 'a little machine for producing conviction in others' (1999: 37). But in general it was geography that formed 'the art whose science was political economy'. Modern space and modern governable spaces were produced by the biological (the laws of population which determine the qualities of the inhabitants) and the economic (the systems of the production of wealth). Governable spaces necessitate the territorialising of governmental thought and practice but are simultaneously produced as differing scales by the cold laws of political economy.

The Nigerian oil complex can be grasped in territorial terms, taking as my cue Nikolas Rose's point about enclosures: 'Governmental thought territorialises itself in different ways...We can analyse the ways in which the idea of a territorially bounded , politically governed nation state under sovereign authority took shape...One can trace anomalous governmental histories of smaller-scale territories...and one can also think of these [as] spaces of enclosure that governmental thought has imagined and penetrated.. .how [does it] happen that social thought territorialises itself on the problem of [for example] the slum in the 19th century?' [Rose 1999: 34-36]. I want to think about the genesis of differing sorts of governable spaces in Nigeria as part of a larger landscape of what Dean calls 'authoritarian governmentality', that is to say an articulation of generalised uses of the instruments of repression with bio-politics. As he says (1999: 209), 'it regards its subjects' capacity for action as subordinate to the expectation of obedience'. I want to root these spaces and forms of power in the logic of petro-capitalist development, that is to say a particular sort of extractive development which is generative of differing sorts of scale, or the 'politics of scale' as Neil Smith (1992) calls it. My analysis conversely charts the relations between oil and violence, but does so through examining how forms of governable (or un-governable) spaces are generated by the baneful twins of authoritarian government and petro-capitalism. To do so, I will turn briefly to governable spaces, and to three in particular that I shall refer to as the space of chieftainship, the space of indigeneity, and the space of the nation state.

Space of Chieftainship

Nembe community in Bayelsa state stands at the originary point of Nigerian oil production. In the 1950s, the Tennessee Oil Company (a US Company) began oil explorations there but oil was not found until much later when Shell D'Arcy unearthed the Oloibiri oil field in Ogbia. Subsequent explorations led to the opening of the large and rich Nembe oil fields near the coast in Okpoama and Twon-Brass axis. Currently, the four Nembe oil fields produce approximately 1,50,000 barrels of high quality petroleum through joint operating agreements between the Nigerian National Petroleum Company (NNPC), AGIP and Shell. If Nembe is the ground zero of oil production, it is also a theatre of extraordinary violence and intra-community conflict, the result of intense competition over political turf and the control of benefits from the oil industry. The violence can be traced back to the late 1980s when the Nembe Council of chiefs acquired power from then king, justice Alagoa Mingi IX, to negotiate royalties and other benefits with the oil companies. The combination of youth-driven violence and intense political competition has transformed Nembe's system of governance and set the stage for further challenges to the traditional authority of chieftainship [Kemedi 2000, HRW 2002].

Oil became commercially viable in 1970s, but to grasp its transformative effects on Nembe politics and community—that is to its genesis as a distinctive governable space—requires an understanding of chieftainship in the delta. Indirect rule in the colonial period certainly left much of the Niger delta marginalised and isolated, but it also, in the name of tradition, built upon and frequently invented chiefly powers of local rule which in the Nembe case were grafted onto a deep and complex structure of kingship and gerontocratic rule. To understand the dynamics of Nembe as a governable space recall that land lay in hands of customary authorities (notwithstanding the fact that the 1969 petroleum law granted the state the power to nationalise all oil resources). Land rights and therefore claims on oil royalties were, from the outset, rooted in the amayanabo (king), and derivatively the subordinate powers, namely, the council of chiefs and the executive council. Historically, the Nembe community possessed a rigid political hierarchy consisting of the amayanabo presiding over, in descending order, the chiefs (or heads of the war canoe houses19) elected by the entire war canoe houses constituted by their prominent sons. Although the chiefs were subservient to the amayanabo, they acted as his closest advisers, supporting him in the event of military threat and, in turn, were responsible for electing the amayanabo from the Mingi group of Houses, or the royal line. The current Nembe council of chiefs is the assemblage of the recognised chiefs of Nembe 'chalked' by the king.

Accordingly, in 1991, the Nembe monarch's ineffectiveness in dealing with the oil companies led to a radical decentralisation of his powers to the council of chiefs, headed by chief Egi Adukpo Ikata. Insofar as the council now dealt directly with Shell, and handled large quantities of money paid by the oil companies, competition for election to the council intensified as various political factions struggled for office. By 2000, the council had expanded from 26 to 90 persons. Coeval with the evisceration of kingly powers, the deepening of the council mandate, and the expansion of the council members, was a subtle process of 'youth mobilisation'. In an age-graded society like the Nembe Ijaw, youth refers to persons typically between their teens and early forties who, whatever achievements they may have obtained (university degrees, fatherhood and so on), remain subservient to their elders. Central to any understanding of the emergence of a militant youth in Nembe town was the catalytic role played by a former company engineer with Elf Oil company named Nimi B P Barigha-Amage. He deployed his knowledge of the oil industry to organise the youths of the Nembe community into a force capable of extracting concessions from the oil companies, in essence, by converting cultural organisation into protection services. Chief Ikata was quick to exploit the awareness and restiveness of the youths to pressure Shell into granting community entitlements. A pact between chief Ikata and the young engineer was in effect instituted; the engineer supplied the youths with information regarding community entitlements, and the chief deployed his knowledge of military logistics to organise the shutting down of flow stations, the seizure of equipment and sabotage [Alagoa 2001, HRW 2002].

Armed with insider knowledge of the companies and an understanding of a loosely defined set of rules regarding company compensation for infringements on community property, Barigha-Amage pushed for the creation of youth 'cultural groups' which gradually, with the support of some members of the council of chiefs, intermediated with oil companies and their liaison officers, and manipulated the system of compensation in the context of considerable juridical and legal ambiguity. Liaison officers, colluding with community representatives, invented ritual or cultural sites that had ostensibly been compromised or damaged by oil operations, for which monies exchanged hands. As the opportunities for appropriating company resources in the name of compensation became visible through the success of the cultural groups, other sections of the youth community began to organise in turn around clan and familial affiliations. In 1994, for example, a group called 'House of Lords' (Isongoforo) was created by a former university lecturer, Lionel Jonathan, and a year later in 1995, the wife of a well-placed military officer, Ituro Garuba established Agbara-fow. Inevitably, with much at stake financially, and control of the space between community and company in the balance, conflicts within and among youth groups proliferated and deepened. In turn, growing community militancy spilled over into often-violent altercations with the much-detested mobile police ('Mopos') and local government authorities. The. regional state and governor attempted to intervene as conditions deteriorated but a government report, on which such action was predicated, was never released for political reasons. A subsequent banning of youth groups had, as a result, no practical effect [HRW 2002].

Slowly, the subversion of royal authority, the strategic alliances between youth and chiefs, and the growing (and armed) conflict between youth groups for access to Shell resulted in the ascendancy of a highly militant Isongoforo. In an environment of rampant insecurity and lawlessness, occupation and closure of flow stations, and tensions between the companies, the service companies and local security forces, Isongoforo was provided 'stand by' payments by the companies (that is to say, it was hired for protection purposes), even as it colluded with the community liaison officers to invent compensations cases. Isongoforo occupied the centre of a new governable space which it ruled through force rather than any sense of consent or customary authority. This quasi-mafia was funded by the large quantities of monies that it commanded from the companies, and by the arms which it controlled. This volatile state of affairs collapsed dramatically as local resentments and struggles proliferated. In February 2000, a 'people's revolution' overthrew Isongoforo, ostensibly precipitated by the humiliation of the council of chiefs at the hands of Shell (backed by the intimidating Isongoforo forces). The chiefs now orchestrated the occupation of flow stations and undermined the powers of Isongoforo by recruiting and supporting other youth groups. By May 2000 Isongoforo had been sent into exile but it was promptly replaced in the wake of Barigha-Amage's return as high chief of Nembe, by his own 'cultural group' henasawo/Teme. Teme instituted a rule of terror and chaos far worse than its predecessors. It too proved unstable in the context of excessive youth mobilisation and split into two factions which subsequently produced two 'counter coups' and much bloodshed. A government peace commission was established in January 2001 in a desperate effort to bring peace to one of the jewels in the oil-producing crown [Alagoa 2001, NDWC 2000].

Much of this later violence (after 1996) could not be regulated by the state authorities because of its concurrence with the 1999 elections in which some of the key youth leaders were expected to deliver votes for the incumbent gubernatorial race. In the creation of what, in effect, was a sort of vigilante rule, there were complex complicities between chiefs, youth groups, local security forces, and the companies. Plans to occupy oil flow stations (for purposes of extortion) were often known in advance and involved collaboration with local company engineers; youths were de facto company employees providing protection services, and local compensation and community officers of Shell and AGIP produced fraudulent compensation cases and entitlements. Nembe, a town with its own long and illustrious history and politics, had become a sort of company town in which authority had shifted from the king to warring factions of youth who were in varying ways in the pay of, and working in conjunction with, the companies. The council of chiefs stood in a contradictory position, seeking to maintain control over revenues from the companies and yet intimidated and undermined by the militant youth groups on whom it depended. In the context of a weak and corrupt state, the genesis of this power nexus bears striking resemblances to the genesis of the Mafia in 19th century Sicily [Blok 1974].

What I have described is the displacement of a specific form of power (chieftainship) by a governable space of civic vigilan-tism, a thickening of civil society that does not necessarily imply the basis of the kind of governance put forth by Granovetter, Putnam and others [Putnam 2000]—that is, the self-organising networks that arise out of the interactions between a variety of organisations and agencies. Civic powers have expanded by overthrowing a territorial system and a gerontocratic royal order. Youth mobilisation—whose political affiliations and ambitions in any case were complex because they reflected an unstable amalgam of clan, family and local electoral loyalties—had thrown up an identity and subject that was indisputably revolutionary, representing an unholy alliance between civic organisations (presenting themselves as cultural organisations) and private companies. Rule in Nembe is a realm of privatised violence, a form of consent by a form of force. Government here turns on what Foucault (2000:208-09) calls 'men in their imbrication with wealth and resources'—the government of men and things, as opposed to territory. It is institutionalised through forms of calculability, techne, and visibility that emerge from the legal and company dispositions to regulate local populations backed by the forces of repression. The governable subject is de facto a sort of employee, and rule is a.Gramscian 'war of position'. Culture serves as the form by which company rule is experienced violent youth groups—but in a way that renders the space increasing ungovernable.

Space of Indigeneity

The Niger delta is a region of considerable, even bewildering, ethifo-linguistic complexity. The eastern region of which the delta is part is dominated statistically by the Ibo majority, but there is a long history of excluded ethnic minorities in the delta dating back at least to the 1950s when the Willinck Commission took note of the inter-ethnic complexity of the region. Throughout the colonial period prior to arrival of commercial oil production, there had been efforts by various minorities, who saw themselves as dominated by the Ibo, to established native authorities of their own. In the 1960s prior to the outbreak of civil war, two charismatic local figures, both Ijaw—Nottingham Dick and Isaac Boro- declared a delta republic, a desperate cry for some sort of political inclusion that lasted a mere 12 days. The ill-fated Delta People's Republic of 1966 was the forerunner of what is now a prairie fire of ethnic mobilisation by the historically excluded minorities—now tagged as 'indigenous' in order to capture the political and legal legitimacy conferred by the International Labour Organisation of the United Nations (ILO 169) [Brysk 2000, Nelson 1999]. The paradigmatic case in the delta is the struggle by Ken Saro-Wiwa and the movement for the survival of the Ogoni people (MOSOP). Their case reveals a rather different sort of governable space, one marked by ethnic subjects and indigenous territory.

The Ogoni are typically seen as a distinct ethnic group, consisting of three subgroups and six clans dotted over 404 sq miles of creeks, waterways and tropical forest', in the north-east fringes of the Niger delta. Located administratively in Rivers State, a Louisiana-like territory of some 50,000 sq km, Ogoniland is one of the most heavily populated zones in all of Africa. The most densely settled areas of Ogoniland—over 1,500 persons per sq km—are also the sites of the largest oil wells. Ogoniland's customary productive base was provided by fishing and agricultural pursuits until the discovery of petroleum, including the huge Bomu field, immediately prior to independence. Part of an enormously complex regional ethnic mosaic, the Ogoni were drawn into internecine conflicts within the delta region, largely as a consequence of the slave trade and its aftermath, in the period prior to arrival of colonial forces at Kono in 1901. The Ogoni resisted the British until 1908 [Naanen 1995] but thereafter were left to stagnate as part of the Opopo division within Calabar province. As Ogoniland was gradually incorporated during the 1930s, the clamour for a separate political division grew at the hands of the first pan-Ogoni organisation, the Ogoni Central Union, which bore fruit with the establishment of the Ogoni native authority in 1947. In 1951, however, the authority was forcibly integrated into the eastern region. Experiencing tremendous neglect and discrimination, integration raised longstanding fears among the Ogoni of Ibo domination. Politically marginalised and economically neglected, the delta minorities feared the growing secessionist rhetoric of the Ibo and consequently led an ill-fated secession of their own in February 1966. Ogoni antipathy to what they saw as a sort of internal colonialism at the hands of the Ibo led to their support of the federal forces during the civil war. While a Rivers State was established in 1967—which compensated in some measure for enormous Ogoni losses during the war—the new state recapitulated in microcosm the larger 'national question'. The new Rivers State was multi-ethnic but presided over by the locally dominant Uaw, for whom the minorities felt little but contempt.

During the first oil boom of the 1970s, Ogoniland's 56 wells accounted for almost 15 per cent of Nigerian oil production and in the past three decades an estimated $ 30 billion in petroleum revenues have flowed from this Lilliputian territory. It was, as local opinion had it, 'Nigeria's Kuwait'.

Yet according to a government commission, Oloibiri, where the first oil was pumped in 1958, has no single kilometre of all-season road and remains 'one of the most backward areas in the country' (cited in Furro 1992: 282, see also Okonta and Douglas 2001). Rivers State saw its federal allocation fall dramatically in absolute and relative terms. At the height of the oil boom, 60 per cent of oil production came from Rivers State but it received only 5 per cent of the statutory allocation (roughly half of that received by Kano, northeastern states and the Ibo heartland, east-central state). Between 1970 and 1980 it received in revenues one 158th of the value of the oil it produced. Few Ogoni households have electricity, there is one doctor per 1,00,000 people, child mortality rates are the highest in the nation, unemployment is 85 per cent, 80 per cent of the population is illiterate and close to half of Ogoni youth have left the region in search of work. Life expectancy is barely 50 years, substantially below the national average. If Ogoniland failed to see the material benefits from oil, what it did experience was an ecological disaster—what the European parliament has called 'an environmental nightmare'. The heart of the geological harms stems from oil spills—either from the pipelines which criss-cross Ogoniland (often passing directly through villages) or from blow-outs at the wellheads—and gas flaring. As regards the latter, a staggering 76 per cent of natural gas in the oil producing areas is flared (compared to 0.6 per cent in the US). As a visiting environmentalist noted in 1993 in the delta, 'some children have never known a dark night even though they have no electricity'. Burning 24 hours per day at temperatures of 13-14,000 degrees Celsius, Nigerian natural gas produces 35 million tonnes of CO_2 and 12 million tonnes of methane, more than the rest of the world (making Nigeria probably the biggest single cause of global warming). The oil spillage record is even worse. There are roughly 300 spills per year in the delta and in the 1970s alone the spillage was four times than the much publicised Exxon Valdez spill in Alaska. In one year alone, almost 7,00,000 barrels were soiled according to a government commission. Ogoniland itself suffered ill-spills between 1985 and 1994. Figures provided by the NNPC document 2,676 spills between 1976 and 1990, 59 per cent of which occurred in Rivers State [Ikein 1990: 171],

38 per cent of which were due to equipment malfunction. Between 1982 and 1992 Shell alone accounted for 1.6 million gallons of spilled oil, 37 per cent of the company's spills worldwide. The consequences of flaring, spillage and waste for Ogoni fisheries and farming have been devastating. Two independent studies completed in 1997 reveal total petroleum hydrocarbons in Ogoni streams at 360 and 680 times the European Community permissible levels [Rainforest Action Network 1997, HRW 1999].

The hanging of Ken Saro-Wiwa and the 'Ogoni Nine' in November 1995—accused of murdering four prominent Ogoni leaders—and the subsequent arrest of 19 others on treason charges, represented the summit of a process of mass mobilisation and radical militancy which had commenced in 1989. MOSOP necessarily built upon previous cultural and political organisations like the Ogoni Klub and Kagote (both elite organisations) and most especially the Ogoni politician Naaku Paul Birabi who established in 1950 the Ogoni state representatives association to promote Ogoni interests in the new eastern region government. The civil war hardened the sense of external dominance among Ogonis. A 'supreme cultural organisation' called Kagote which consisted largely of traditional rulers and high-ranking functionaries, was established at the war's end and in turn gave birth in 1990 to MOSOP. A new strategic phase began in 1989 with a programme of mass action and passive resistance on the one hand and a renewed effort to focus on the environmental consequences of oil (and Shell's role in particular) and on group rights within the federal structure. Animating the entire struggle was, in Leton's words, the 'genocide being committed in the dying years of the 20th century by multinational companies under the supervision of the government' (cited in Naanen 1995: 66). A watershed moment in MOSOP's history. was the drafting in 1990 of an Ogoni Bill of Rights [Saro-Wiwa 1992]. Documenting a history of neglect and local misery, the Ogoni Bill took head on the question of Nigeria federalism and minority rights. Calling for participation in the affairs of the republic as 'a distinct and separate entity', the Bill outlined a plan for autonomy and self-determination in which there would be guaranteed 'political control of Ogoni affairs by

Ogoni people...the right to control and use a fair proportion of Ogoni economic resources...(and) adequate representation as of right in all Nigerian national institutions' [Saro-Wiwa 1990:11]. Inshort, the Bill of Rights addressed the question of the unit to which revenues should be allocated -and derivatively the rights of minorities [HRW 1999, Okonta 2002]. At the heart of Saro-Wiwa's vision was an Ogoni state.

In spite of the remarkable history of MOSOP between 1990 and 1996, its ability to represent itself as a unified pan-Ogoni organisation remained an open question. There is no pan-Ogoni myth of origin (characteristic of some delta minorities), and a number of the Ogoni subgroups (clans) engender stronger local loyalties than any affiliation to Ogoni 'nationalism'. Gokana clan for example was the most populous and well-educated and its elites wielded disproportionate influence in Ogoni. Conversely, the Eleme clan-head did not even sign the Ogoni Bill of Rights and Eleme's leading historian has argued that they are not in fact Ogoni [Ngofa 1988]. In 1994, Eleme leaders proposed the creation of Nchia state which comprised non-Ogonis from Bonny, Andoni, Opobo and Etche, thereby turning their backs on Saro-Wiwa's goal [Okonta 2003]. Furthermore, the MOSOP leaders were actively opposed by elements of the traditional clan leadership, by prominent leaders and civil servants in state government, and by some critics who felt Saro-Wiwa was out to gain 'cheap popularity' [Osgahae 1995: 334]. Some Ogoni notables (Edward Kobani, Leton) aspired to participate in conventional politics by running for the two major parties rather than assisting in the birth of a nation. MOSOP, moreover, was a political movement of the elite led by the elite; it was not a mass movement and youth and women were not represented on its first steering committee. Gradually the youth wing of MOSOP, which Saro-Wiwa had used, emerged as militants but the leadership was often incapable of controlling it. MOSOP, in short, was wrecked by tensions. There were as Okonta says 'cracks in the pot' (2003: 12).

Saro-Wiwa built upon over 50 years of Ogoni organising and upon three decades of resentment against the oil companies, to provide a mass base and a youth-driven radicalism—and an international visibility—capable of challenging state power. Yet at its core the indigenous subject—and the indigenous space—was contentious and problematic. Ike Okonta (2002) has brilliantly shown, how in the Ogoni case, indigeneity unravelled into fragments of class, clan, generation and gender. These tensions came to the fore after Saro-Wiwa's death and MOSOP declined as rapidly as it had ascended.

What sort of articulation of indigenous identity and political subjectivity did Saro-Wiwa pose? What sort of governable space did Ogoniland represent? It was clearly one in which territory and oil were the building blocks upon which ethnic difference and indigenous rights were constructed. And yet it was an unstable and contradictory sort of articulation. First, there was no simple sense of 'Ogoniness', no unproblematic unity, and no singular form of political subject (despite Saro-Wiwa's claim that 98 per cent of Ogonis supported him). MOSOP itself had at least five somewhat independent internal strands embracing youth, women, traditional rulers, teachers and churches. It represented a fractious and increasing divided 'we', as the splits and conflicts between Saro-Wiwa and other elite Ogoni confirms (Ogoni Crisis 1996).27 Second, Saro-Wiwa constantly invoked Ogoni culture and tradition yet he also argued that war and internecine conflict had virtually destroyed the fabric of Ogoni society by 1900 (1992: 14). His own Utopia then rested on the recreation of Ogoni culture and suffered like all Mr-histories from a quasi-mythic invocation of the past. Third, ethnicity was the central problem of post-colonial Nigeria—the corruption of ethnic majorities—and for Saro-Wiwa its panacea (the multiplication of ethnic minority power). To invoke the history of exclusion and the need for ethnic minority inclusion as the basis for federalism, led Saro-Wiwa to ignore the histories and geographies of conflict and struggle among and between ethnic minorities. Saro-Wiwa's brilliance, then, was to make MOSOP a green, indigenous movement (with international backing and visibility) and to take the movement to the poor and the young to secure a powerful identity, in the face of elite opposition (and his own marginal position in the 1980s). Saro-Wiwa's crowning glory was Ogoni national day on

January 4, 1993 when he presided over the birth of the Ogoni flag, the Ogoni anthem and the National Youth Council of the Ogoni People.

Paradoxically MOSOP surfaced as a foundational indigenous movement even though Ogoni's significance as an oil-producing region was diminishing. By the late 1990s moreover as a movement it had fallen apart and inter-group struggles deprived it of much of its previous momentum and visibility. But it gave birth to what one might call indigenous movements among oil producing communities. The same forces have spawned a raft of self-determination indigenous movements among Ijaw (INC, IYV), Isoko (IDU), Urhobo (UPU), Itsekiri (INP), Ogbia (MORETO) among others [Obi 2001]. MOSOP itself fell apart precisely as these other movements gained power. Since the return to civilian rule in 1999, there has been a rash of such minority movements across the delta calling for 'resource control', autonomy and a national sovereign conference to rewrite the Nigerian constitution. At the same time the delta has become ever more engulfed in civil strife: militant occupations of oil flow stations, pipeline sabotage, intra-urban ethnic violence, and the near-anarchy of state security operating in tandem with company security forces. The shock troops of many of these indigenous movements are youth and women, and the multiplication of ethnic youth movements is one of the most important political developments in contemporary Nigeria. And it is here that the politics of oil-producing communities meet up with the politics of oil-producing indigenous groups.

What does the Ogoni case reveal, then, as a governable space? Particular 'populations' have been constructed as indigenous. As I explain below, this construction emerged from the nationalist struggle as customary rights were added to a discourse of citizenship. But the process received enormous energy as indigeneity as a political category garnered international support in the last part of the 20th century, a resource that Saro-Wiwa deployed brilliantly [Bob 2002].

The emergence of a national debate in Nigeria over resource control in the late 1990s is precisely a product of indigenous claims-making on the state, a process by which ethnic identifications must be discursively and politically produced.

The Ogoni case shows that there is no pre-given ethnic identity, but complex and unstable genealogies of identification that have emerged in the last century [Li 1996]. The indigene has to be made—interpolated—around a strong sense of territory and tradition but in the context of cultural, economic and political heterogeneity. This was achieved through an imbrication of things and people—oil and ethnicity—and it has been generative of a profusion of indigenous movements. Indigeneity has in this sense unleashed the huge political energies of ethnic minorities who recapitulate in some respects the post-colonial history of spoils politics in Nigeria, The effect of this multi-ethnic mobilisation was the production of political and civic organisations and new forms of governable space, a veritable jigsaw of militant particularisms. The Kaiama Declaration in 1999 indicates that there is a pan-ethnic solidarity movement in the works, but its contours are at present limited [Douglas and Okonta 2001, ERA 1999]. As the Ogoni case shows, much of this visibility and identification turned on the invention and reinvention of tradition and local knowledge, with an eye to the Nigerian constitution and international politics [Nelson 1999]. This is a case of the multiplication of governable spaces which stand in some tension or even contradiction with each other—they account for the explosion of inter-ethnic tensions in the delta—and within the national space of Nigeria, to which I now turn.

Space of Nationalism

One of the striking aspects of the governable spaces of indigeneity as they emerge in the delta is that they become vehicles for political claims, typically articulated as the need for a local government or in some cases a state. Indigeneity necessarily raises the question of a third governable space, that of the nation state, an entity that pre-existed oil and came to fruition in 1960 at independence. Oil in this sense became part of the nation-building process—the creation of an 'oil nation'. Nature and nationalism become inextricably linked. But how did petro-capitalism—understood as a state-led, and thoroughly globalised, development strategy—stand in relation to the creation of the governable space called modern Nigeria?

As Mamood Mamdani (1996,2001) has observed, colonial rule and decentralised despotism were synonymous. The native authorities consolidated local class power in the name of tradition (ethnicity) and sustained a racialised view of civic rights. The nationalist movement had two wings, a radical and a mainstream. Both wished to deracialise civic rights but the latter won out and reproduced the dual legacy of colonialism. They provided civic rights for all Nigerians, but a bonus 'customary rights' for indigenous people. The country had to decide which ethnic groups were indigenous and which were not a basis for political representation, a process that became constitutionally mandated in Nigeria. Federal institutions are quota-driven for each state but only those indigenous to the state may apply for a quota. As Mamdani (1998: 7) puts it:

The effective elements of the federation are neither territorial units called states nor ethnic groups but ethnic groups with their own states.. .Given this federal character every ethnic group compelled to seek its own home its NA, its own state. With each new political entity the non-indigenes continues to grow.

Once law enshrines cultural identity as the basis for political identity, it necessarily converts ethnicity into a political force. As a consequence, in Nigeria, clashes in the postcolonial period were ethnic, and such ethnic clashes, which dominated the political landscape in the last three decades, are always at root about customary rights to land and, derivatively, to a local government or to a state that can empower those on the ground as ethnically indigenous.

Into this mix enters oil, that is to say a valuable, centralised (state-owned) resource. It is a national resource on which citizenship claims can be constructed. As much as the state uses oil to build a nation and to develop, so communities use oil wealth to activate community claims on what is seen popularly as unimaginable wealth—black gold. The governable space of Nigeria is as a consequence re-territorialised through ethnic claims-making [Suberu 2001, Adebayo 1993]. The result is that access to oil revenues amplifies what I call sub-national political institution-making; politics becomes then a massive state-making machine. This partly explains how, between 1966 and the present, the number of local governments has grown from 50 to almost 1000, and the number of states from 3 to 36! Nigeria as a modern nation state has become a machine for the production of ever more local political institutions. The logic is ineluctable and terrifying.

What sort of national governable space emerges from such multiplication in which, incidentally, the political entities called states or local government areas (LGAs) become vehicles for massive corruption and fraud—or the disposal of oil revenues? The answer is that it works against precisely the creation of an imagined community of the sort that Benedict Anderson (1998) saw as synonymous with nationalism. Nation-building, whatever its style of imaging, rests in its modern form on a sort of calculation, integration, and state and bureaucratic rationality which the logic of rent-seeking, petro-corruption, ethnic spoils politics, and state multiplication works to systematically undermine. Lauren Berlant has said that every nation—and hence every governable national space—requires a 'national symbolic'; a national fantasy which 'designates how national culture becomes local through images, narratives and movements which circulate in the personal and collective unconsciousness' (1991: 61). My point is that the Nigerian national symbolic grew weaker and more attenuated as a result of the political economy of oil. There was no sense of the national fantasy at the local level; it was simply a big pocket of oil monies to be raided in the name of indigeneity. At independence, Obafemi Awolowo, the great western Nigerian politician, said that Nigeria was not a nation but a 'mere geographical expression'. Forty years later this is still true.

What we have in other words is not nation-building—understood in the sense of a governable space—but perhaps its reverse: the 'unimagining' or deconstruction of a particular sense of national community. Nicos Poulantzas (1978) said that national or modern unity requires a historicity of a territory and a territorialisation of a history. Oil capitalism (and its attendant governmentality) in Nigeria has achieved neither of these requirements. The 'fictional' governable space called Nigeria was always something of a public secret. Forty years of post-colonial rule has made this secret both more public as ethnic segregation has continued unabated and undermined the very idea of the production of governable subjects. The double-movement of petro-capitalism within the frame of a modern nation state has eviscerated the governable space of the nation; it has compromised it and worked against a sense of governable subject. The same, incidentally, might be said of the impact of oil on the Muslim communities of Nigeria [Watts 1998: 2000]. Oil and identity—people and things—have produced an unimagined community on which the question of Nigeria's future hangs.

Blood and Oil

The entire history of petroleum is, as Daniel Yergin (1991) details in his encyclopaedic Whig account of the industry The Prize, replete with criminality, violence and the worst of frontier capitalism. Graft, autocratic thuggery, and the most grotesque exercise of imperial power are its hallmarks. As the US armoured divisions roll up the Iraqi oil corridor around Basra, this point hardly needs further empirical confirmation. And it is to be expected in an age of unprecedented denationalisation and market liberalisation—to say nothing of the horrific rise of the gas-guzzling sports utility vehicle in the US—the mad scramble to locate the next petrolic El Dorado continues unabated. Eastern Russia looks ever more like a slice of Mafiosi sovereignty. Petro-violence is rarely off the front pages of the press. The Caspian basin reaching from the borders of Afghanistan to the Russian Caucasus is a repository of enormous petro-wealth; Turkmenistan, Kazakhstan, Azerbaijan, Georgia and the southern Russian provinces (Ossetia, Dagestan, Chechnya) have however become, in the wake of the collapse of the Soviet Union, a 'zone of civil conflict and war'. The oil companies jockey for position in an atmosphere of frontier vigilantism and what the Azerbaijani president calls 'armed conflict, aggressive separatism and nationalism'.

Based on the Nigerian case, I have suggested that petro-capitalism operates through a particular sort of oil complex (a configuration of firm, state and community). The complex is strongly territorial, operating through local oil concessions. The presence and activities of the oil companies as part of the oil complex constitute a challenge to forms of community authority, inter-ethnic relations, and local state institutions principally through the property and land disputes that are engendered, and via forms of popular mobilisation and agitation to gain access to: *(i)* company rents and compensation revenues, and *(ii)* the petro-revenues of the Nigerian state largely through the creation of regional and/or local state institutions. The complex generates differing sorts of governable spaces in which contrasting identities and forms of rule come into play; in some cases youth and generational forces are key, in some cases gender, in others the clan or the kingdom or the ethnic minority (or indigenous peoples), in some cases local chiefly or governmental authorities, and in others the forces of the local state. A striking aspect of contemporary development in Nigeria is the simultaneous production of differing forms of rule and governable space—different politics of scale [Smith 1992]—all products of similar forces and yet which work against, and often stand in direct contradiction to one another. I have focused on youth, the indigene or ethnic minority, and the nation. These idioms are inseparable from oil, but their forms of identification and the robustness of their spaces are often incompatible. Standing at the centre of each governable space is a contradiction: at the oil community, the overthrowing of gerontocratic authority but its substitution by a sort of violent Mafia youthful rule. At the level of the ethnic community is the tension between civic nationalism and a sort of exclusi vist militant particularism. And at the level of the nation, one sees the contradiction between oil-based state centralisation and state fragmentation, or multiplication, as oil becomes a sort of generalised equivalent put to the service of massive corruption. I have tried to root these contradictions in the double-movement of petro-çapitalism which is generative of an authoritarian governmentality constituted by the three forms of governable space that I have described. Such is the heart of the so-called crisis of the post-colonial state in Africa. It is in this sense that I invoke the idea of 'economies of violence' to characterise governmentality in contemporary Nigeria.

7

Natural Resources in Capitalist Frontiers

A frontier is an edge of space and time: a zone of not yet not yet mapped, 'not yet' regulated. It is a zone of unmapping: even in its planning, a frontier is imagined as unplanned. Frontiers are not just discovered at the edge; they are projects in making geographical and temporal experiences. Their' wildness is' made of visions and vines and violence; it is both material and imaginative. Frontiers reach backward as well as forward in time energising old fantasies, even as they embody their impossibilities. On the resource frontier, the small and the great collaborate and collide in a climate of chaos and violence. They wrest landscape elements from previous livelihoods and ecologies to turn them into wild resources, available for the industries of the world.

Most descriptions of resource frontiers take the existence of resources for granted. Most descriptions label and count the resources and tell us who owns what. The landscape itself appears inert: ready to be dismembered and packaged for export. In contrast, the challenge I have set myself is to make the landscape a lively actor. Landscapes are simultaneously natural and social, and they actively shift and turn in the interplay of human and non-human practices. Frontier landscapes are particularly active: hills are flooding away, streams are stuck in mud, vines swarm over fresh stumps, ants and humans are on the move. On the frontier, nature goes wild.

The place I describe is a mountainous, forested strip of southeast Kalimantan. My companions in travelling and learning this landscape are Meratus Dayaks, old inhabitants of the area, whose livelihood has been based on shifting cultivation and forest foraging. For Meratus, the frontier has come as a shock and a disruption; it is with their help that I experience the trauma of transformation. There are other perspectives: for some, such as migrants and miners, the frontier is an opening full of promise. They come in expectation of resources, and so they can ignore how these resources are traumatically produced. I leave their stories for other chronicles, of which there are many.

In the mid-1990s, the political regime in Indonesia was called the New Order. The New Order was a centralised and repressive political machine that depended heavily on the power of its military, particularly to control the countryside. In the 1970s and 1980s, the regime flourished through a rhetoric of state-led development. In the 1990s, however, privatisation became a regime watchword; in practice, the new policies further concentrated economic power in the hands of the president's family and close cronies. In Kalimantan, state policy privileged corporate control of natural resources; huge tracts were assigned to logging companies, mining companies, and pulp-and-paper as well as oil palm plantation companies. The military played an important role in transferring these tracts from previous residents to their corporate owners; military men also took their own interest in resources. It seems fair to say that the military had a central role in creating the 'wildness' of the frontier. This seminal period, which has gone on to shape the wildness of the early 21st century, is the moment I describe.

An Abandoned Logging Road

An abandoned logging road has got to be one of the most desolate places on earth. By definition, it does not go anywhere. If you are walking there, it is either because you are lost or you are trespassing, or both. The wet clay builds clods on your boots, if you have any, sapping your strength, and if you don't have any boots, the sun and the hot mud are merciless. Whole hillsides shift beside you, sliding into the stagnant pools where mosquitoes breed. Abandoned roads soon lose their shape, forcing you in and out of eroded canyons and over muddy trickles where bridges once stood but are now choked by loose soil, vines crawling on disinterred roots and trunks sliding, askew. Yet, ironically, the forest as a site of truth and beauty seems clearer from the logging road than anywhere else, since it is the road that slices open the neat cross section in which underbrush, canopy, and high emergent trees are so carefully structured.

In 1994,1 walked on a lot of abandoned logging roads in the eastern sector of South Kalimantan, Indonesia, between the Meratus Mountains and the coastal plains now covered with transmigration villages—block A, block B, Block C—and giant, miles-square plantations of oil palm, rubber, and Acacia for the pulp and paper trade. The region was transformed from when I had last seen it in the 1980s. Then, despite the logging, I had thought the forest might survive; local villagers were asserting customary resource rights and transmigration here was just a gleam in one engineer's eye, and he wasn't in charge. Now, even beyond the newly-planted industrial tree plantations lay miles of scrub and vines. These were landslides of slippery red and yellow clay, with silted-up excuses for water. The logging roads had eroded into tracks for motorcycles, water buffalo, and the still-streaming mass of immigrant and local blood and sweat that the government calls 'wild': wild loggers, wild miners, and bands of roving entrepreneurs and thieves. I had seen resource booms before: When the prices for rattan shot up in the 1980s, for example, people went crazy cutting rattan until all the rattan had been cut to the ground. But this was something different. Something easily called degradation was riding through the land. It was the kind of scene that informs so many powerful theories of resource management. The human presence was leaving the landscape all but bare. This, they say, is ordinary behaviour on the resource frontier where everything is plentiful and wild. It is human nature, they say, and the nature of resources.

In the violent clarity of the abandoned logging road, questions come to mind that might seem simple or even idiotic elsewhere. How does nature at the frontier become a set of resources? How are landscapes made empty and wild so that anyone can come to use and claim them? How do ordinary people get involved in destroying their environments, even their own home places?

This is business that gets inside our daily habits and our dreams. Two complementary nightmares come into being; the frontier emerges in the intertwined attraction and disgust of their engagement. Consider in comparison the urban frontiers of southern California. Orange County is full of planned communities, industrial tree plantations of neatly spaced condominiums, row on row on row, which give way only to identical roads and shopping malls. There is truly no directions, no place marks, only faceless serenity, time on hold. Orange County is one kind of nightmare. Its flip side is south-central Los Angeles, the mere thought of which drives masses of whites and Asian Americans behind the Orange Curtain. Time is not on hold in that bastion of short lives. Yet these two nightmares play with each other: Just as the fear of hell drives the marketing schemes of paradise, so too does the desire of paradise fuel the schemes of hell. Both rise and fall on the spectacular performances of savvy entrepreneurs.

The same is true in Kalimantan. The giant monocrop plantations are the flip side of the wild resource frontier: on one side, endless rows of silent symmetry and order, bio-power applied to trees; on the other side, wild loggers, miners, and villagers in the raucous, sped-up time of looting. Each calls the other into existence. Each solves the problems put in motion by the other. Each requires the same entrepreneurial spirit. In that spirit, gold nuggets, swallows' nests, incense wood, ironwood posts, great logs destined to be plywood, and whole plantations of future pulp are conjured. Here I find the first answer to my impertinent questions. Resources are made by 'resourcefulness' in both plantation and wild frontier. The activity of the frontier is to make human subjects as well as natural objects.

The frontier, indeed, had come to Kalimantan. It had not always been there. Dutch plantation schemes mainly bypassed Kalimantan in the colonial period, allowing colonial authorities to treat their natives as subjects of kingdoms and cultures. Kalimantan's Dayaks, to them patently uncivilised, were still seen as having law and territorial boundaries, not a wilderness that needed to be filled up. In its first years the post-colonial nation maintained Kalimantan's villages, fields, and forests. Commercial logging only got underway in the 1970s. Administrative expansion and resettlement followed, with the goal of homogenising the nation. In the 1980s, conflicts broke out between village people and commercial loggers. Massive fires and waves of immigration disrupted emergent localisms. Through the 1980s, however, it was possible to see rural Kalimantan as a landscape of villages, small cultivations, and traditional agro-forestry, with discrete patches of estate agriculture and large-scale logging and mining here and there.

The late 1980s and 1990s witnessed a national wave of entre-preneurship. Spurred on by economic 'liberalisation' with its international sponsors, and a consolidating regional capitalism, entrepreneurs shot up at every level from conglomerates to peasant tour guides. In this great surge of resourcefulness Kalimantan became a frontier.

The frontier, then, is not a natural or indigenous category. It is a travelling theory, a blatantly foreign form requiring translation. It arrived with many layers of previous associations. 'Indonesian Miners Revive Gold Rush Spirit of 49ers', proclaimed a headline in the *Los Angeles Times*? Indonesian frontiers were shaped to the model of other wild times and places. Nor was 1849 California the only moment of frontier-making available to be reworked and revived. There is the dark Latin American frontier: a place of violence, conflicting cultures, and an unforgiving nature driving once-civilised men to barbarism, as Domingo Sarmiento, soon to be president of Argentina, argued in 1845. This savage vision of the frontier has continued to percolate through later frontier optimism. There is the nation-making frontier, as famously articulated by Frederick Jackson Turner in his 1893 address.

'The Significance of the Frontier in American History'. Wild, empty spaces are said to have inspired white men to national democracy and freedom in the US. Amazing for its erasures, the power of this formulation is suggested by the fact that US historians remained in its thrall for nearly a hundred years. Finally, in the 1960s, frontier chroniclers dared to mention that there were Native Americans, Asians, Hispanics, and women in these empty spaces, and they may not have benefited from that nation-making freedom quite so much as Anglo-American men. Finally, in the 1980s, environmental historians dared mention that someone despoiled the land, forests, and rivers. But the proud frontier story of the making of 'America' will probably be around a long time, particularly because it was remade in an internationally colonising form after the Second World War in the concept of the techno-frontier, the endless frontier made possible by industrial technology. The closing of national borders, dense settlement, and resource scarcity need no longer lead to frontier nostalgia; the techno-frontier is always open and expanding. In the guise of development, the dream of the techno-frontier hit Indonesian centres hard in the late 1960s. By the 1990s, it had dragged its older frontier cousins, those entangled stories of the wild, to the rural peripheries.

Frontiers are notoriously unstable, and it is fitting that Kalimantan landscapes should have a role in forging new frontier conceptions. The frontier arrived in Kalimantan after environmentaiism had already become established not just among activists but also among government bureaucrats and corporate public relations agents. No one could be surprised this time to find that frontier-making is destructive of forests and indigenous cultures. Susanna Hecht and Alexander Cockburn write that in the Amazon, heroic development plans unexpectedly turned to smoke, mud, and violence: 'The generals had unleashed forces beyond their control, and now the Amazon faced its apocalypse'. But in New Order Kalimantan, the Amazon apocalypse was already known. Plans were set in motion to save the environment in the process of destroying it. Tree plantations were introduced to restore deforested and degraded land. Only then was the landscape deforested and degraded to make way for the restorative tree plantations. Giant mining conglomerates were licensed to save the land from the pollution and depreciations of wild miners, yet legal and illegal prospectors were inseparable. "They go where we go", a Canadian engineer explained, "and sometimes we follow them". The national timber king, also czar of plywood and crown prince of mines, hosted the 10K 'Run for the Rainforest' and produced a glossy coffee-table book of disappearing species. This is the salvage frontier, where making, saving, and destroying resources are utterly mixed up, where zones of conservation, production, and resource sacrifice overlap almost fully, and canonical time frames of nature's study, use, and preservation are reversed, conflated, and confused.

By this point it should be clear that by frontier I don't mean a place or even a process but an imaginative project capable of moulding both places and processes. Turner describes the frontier as "the meeting point between savagery and civilisation". It is a site of transformations; "the wilderness masters the colonist. ... Little by little he masters the wilderness..." It is a space of desire: it calls; it appears to create its own demands; once glimpsed, one cannot but explore and exploit it. Frontiers have their own technologies of space and time. Their emptiness is expansive, spreading across the land; they draw the quick, erratic temporality of rumour, speculation, and cycles of boom and bust, encouraging ever-intensifying forms of resourcefulness. On the Kalimantan salvage frontier, frontier intensification and proliferation lurch forward in a hall of mirrors, becoming showy parodies of themselves. Time moves so quickly that results precede their causes, and the devastation expected behind the line of frontier expansion suddenly appears, as it seems, ahead of its advance.

The Kalimantan frontier is not the enactment of a principle of commodification or conquest. The commodification of forest products is centuries old in this area, and while the new frontier draws on the earlier trade, it is not a logical intensification of this earlier trade. The frontier is not a philosophy but rather a series of historically nonlinear leaps and skirmishes that pile together to create their own intensification and proliferation. The most helpful scholarship, then, is not to be found in abstract treatises but rather in historical descriptions and ethnographies. Thus, accounts of the US west tell us how the rush to grab one landscape element can jump off into another, as when gold prospectors made property claims on stream water. Legal precedents unexpectedly link one region and another. Aesthetic models are carried to new homes, as colonial conservation inspired the national parks movement.

As these kinds of moves are repeated, they gain a cultural productiveness even in their quirky unpredictability. Thus Marianne Schmink and Charles Wood describe frontiers in Amazonia as a series of ironic twists. "Planned communities lead to unplanned settlement; resource nationalisation leads to private control, land titling leads to forgery, military protection leads to generalised violence." Such twists are more than irony: they predict and perform their own reversals, forming productive confusions and becoming models for other frontiers. In Kalimantan, related paradoxes produce frontier degradation and salvage. The frontier is made in the shifting terrain between legality and illegality, public and private ownership, brutal rape and passionate charisma, ethnic collaboration and hostility, violence and law, restoration and extermination.

Legal, Illegal

Shifting cultivation is illegal in Indonesia, despite the fact that it is the major subsistence technology for many rural people in Kalimantan, including Meratus Dayaks. Perhaps that is why, as I hiked down the Meratus Mountains into the eastern coastal plains with Meratus friends, the lines of legality were not clear to me, and I was hardly aware that the immigrant loggers I passed were out of bounds, wild men. As soon as we hit the old logging roads we found them, singly or in groups of three or four, each with a small chainsaw or a water buffalo to haul out the logs. Their living places were bed-sized bamboo platforms along the road with only a sheet of plastic hung over to keep out the rain; they seemed to have no possessions but a coffee pot and a can of mackerel, the poor man's sardines. We stopped to drink sticky thick coffee, loaded with sugar, and to talk of the pleasures and dangers of the forest world they knew. They chanted the prices of wood, the names of logs. They spooked themselves, and us, with tales of stolen chainsaws and armed men on the roads. They were always planning to leave in a few days, when the earnings looked good, and before fiercer men arrived. Even as quick-moving transients, they gave us a human face for the frontier.

My friends thought the men worked for Inhutani, a government forest company, and while this turned out to be technically wrong, they were right that the lines between public, private, and criminal enterprise were unclear. These loggers have both legitimacy and access. They sell their logs to the properly concessioned logging companies or to small construction firms. Where environmental regulations keep the companies off mountain slopes or village claims push them back, that's where the wild loggers go. They fill out logging economies of scale, and their earnings are the only prosperity that logging is likely to bring to the province. Their chainsaws come to them through networks of renting and profit-sharing that cross local, ethnic, and religious lines. They form the slender end of channels of capital reaching from rich Chinese entrepreneurs, conglomerates, and—at that time—the family of the president, flowing in ever narrowing channels out into the forest. Usually, the police and the army do not bother them, although the police and the army can be unpredictable. Many pay fees to official Meratus village heads to give them permission to cut in village forests, and while villagers complain that village heads keep it all for themselves, this privatisation is common, even proper, for government village subsidies.

And yet, both, despite and because of all this respectability, these lonely loggers carried and spread the 'wildness' of the frontier. Even in sitting with them, chatting with them, we partook of that wildness. They encouraged our fears of armed men; oh, no one will attack you, they joked, because they will assume you are carrying a lot of guns. And who can tell the difference between a logger and an armed thief? Each time we came upon another man, another logger/thief, we stopped, hoping to domesticate him with our chatter. Perhaps he wouldn't attack us; perhaps he would alert us to the presence of other logger/thieves. Soon our nerves were jangling from all those cups of coffee, and by then we had formed a silent pack, each huddling in his or her own unspoken fear.

They modelled frontier behaviour for us, teaching us the value of wood until my Meratus companions began looking at familiar forest trees with eyes like cash registers. Oh, that one could bring me a million rupiah, Ma Salam sighed, interrupting our conversation about environmentalism. In writing their names or initials on the logs they cut, the wild loggers had introduced the new practice in this area of writing one's name on trees—to claim the tree to hold it or sell it to a logger with a chainsaw before someone else did. The proliferation of naming brought new identities for trees and men, wrapping both in fearless assertion and violence, for, people said, armed men came by and cut the name off the tree, or cut the tree above the mark, and wrote their own names on the logs. If you confront them with five men, my friends said, they will come at you with 10 or 20. Sell quickly and move on to write your name again.

Who were these men, so human and yet so transiently identified? They came from everywhere and spoke the common language of trade and calculation based on the hope of a quick windfall. They were called penyingso, 'chainsaw men', or pembaluk, 'square log men', after the shape of their logs. No one knew them as wild, but they were men without ordinary culture. Appendages to their equipment and their products, they had names but no houses, families, meals, work schedule, or ordinary time. And in this stripped-down human form, they communicated across cultures, arranging ethnic collaborations. They offered a hot human connection to still the chills of fear. This thrilling connection was an anaesthetic, blocking out the damaged world in which they operated—a world already left behind by bigger frontier makers, the soil sloughing off the hills, trees falling, waters muddied. Looking in and through that damaged world, can't you see the resources waiting to be claimed?

It is difficult to find the words to discuss this kind of transethnic, translocal collaboration and the regional resource dynamics it sets in motion. Resource economists and bureaucrats recognise no localisms; to them, the world is a frontier. There is no point in asking how frontiers come to be; they are nature itself. To counter that perspective, anthropologists, rural sociologists, and geographers have drawn attention to non-frontier-like (or even anti-frontier) environmental social forms, such as common property, community management, and indigenous knowledge. They have returned attention to the cultural specificity of capitalism and state bureaucracy. This important and quite wonderful work has come to dominate local and regional analyses of environment and society in Kalimantan; scholars point to the long-term social making of the rainforest, to a community 'ethic of access' that sustains forest commodities, and to the bizarre stereotypes of government planners. My own work has developed within this dialogue.

Yet in contrasting community conventions with state and corporate schemes, there is little room for discussing the call of the wild, with its regionwide collaborations for aggressive resource grabbing and the seemingly-unstoppable spread of the frontier. One might call this 'the tragedy of the tragedy of the commons', that is, the tragic result of state and corporate policies that assume and enforce open-access conventions as the flip side and precondition of private property. By refusing to recognise alternative forms of access, these policies will alternatives to disappearance. But this is a tragedy that cannot be well described with the vocabulary of management, property, and access rules. From the perspective of the abandoned logging roads, the divide between community and state-corporate standards feels nostalgic: too little, too late. The logging road and its illegal-legal loggers from everywhere call me toward more dangerous country.

One look back: grand schemes never fully colonise the territories upon which they are imposed. If the frontier is an environmental project, not a place, it can never fill the landscape. Away from the logging road, there are trees, fields, and villages, and not everyone is so caught up in frontier schemes. The frontier could move on, and something else could happen in its place. The forest might regenerate. Although...those industrial tree plantations are truly huge, and through them the frontier claims powerful national and international players.

The Public Private

Riding from the provincial capital up the east coast and in toward the mountains in an airless, overcrowded van with the music so loud it closes down my senses, there is more than enough anaesthetic; yet the difference between legal resource concessions and the wild is perfectly visible here. The road runs for miles through land without underbrush or animal life but only neatly planted tree stock, row on row on row. The transmigration villages recently placed here to provide the labour force for these future trees are similarly orderly, blank, and anonymous; in striking contrast to everywhere else I've been in Indonesia, the passengers get on and off at these nameless stops without looking at us or speaking. Sometimes we stop in noisy frontier towns, full of gold merchants, truckers, and hungry, aggressive men. But soon enough we are back among the silent army of young trees. This is the kind of discipline that boosted Indonesia—for awhile—among the so-called Asian dragons. In the name of political stability, discipline made economic indicators soar.

Appearances are important here. No weeds, no trash timber. Indeed, it is unclear to what extent appearances were not the New Order economy's most important product. Oil palm, the darling of the export-crop set, was sponsored by foreign and domestic plantation subsidies; perhaps the companies will have moved on before the oil is pressed. The pulp plantations were financed by the national reforestation programme, the answer to environmentalists' concern for the rainforest. New international agreements offered plantation timber as the solution to rainforest destruction; timber companies put in plantations, sponsored by the government, to earn the right to cut down more forest, useful for future plantations. Meanwhile the young trees await future pulp factories. And as they wait, what will befall them? Many of the Acacias are cloned from the same parent stock, making them highly vulnerable to disease. They are also affected by a rot that causes hollow boles, an apt image for an economy of appearances.

There were government corporations here, and there were private ones, but most fell awkwardly across this distinction. In 1994, the oil palms were said to belong to the wife of then president Suharto, Mrs. Tien Suharto, who died in 1996 but before her death was widely parodied as Mrs. Tien (Ten) Per cent, after her voracious interest in the economy. The loggers told villagers who complained about the invasion of village forests to 'go ask Mrs Tien'. The president's family served both a material and a mythical role in the plantation economy. The capital they controlled was both public and private. And it was the confusion of these categories that allowed frontier investment to flourish. For whom were these resources discovered and developed: national interest, the army, the president, foreign corporations, or, perhaps, all of the above?

Even the staunchest of neoclassical economists admit that it was difficult to distinguish among domestic, foreign, and government ownership in New Order Indonesia, given the mix of investors, the central importance of patronage, and the slippage back and forth between military and private enterprise. The confusion proliferated at every level. Foreign was domestic: foreign aid formed a major portion of domestic revenue, and foreign firms worked through domestic partners. Public was private: the explicit goal of the government was to sponsor entrepreneurship at every level. Even peasant subsidies in the 1990s were individual entrepreneurship loans. Licences and concessions were both public and private. Civil servants were paid a low base salary and expected to gain the rest of their living from perks and benefits of their discretionary authority.

You could call this corruption, or you could call it, as one North American corporate executive, gracefully submitting to government demands for a share of his company's enterprise, dubbed it, 'Indonesia's political, economic, and social environment'. One must also consider these public-private arrangements in relation to the worldwide post-cold war infatuation with the market. Soon after the collapse of the Soviet Union in 1989, every nation state redoubled its endorsement of the market, or at least the appearance of the market, and New Order Indonesia was exemplary. The bureaucracy was the market; its goal was to promote entrepreneurship. The military was the market; generals and common soldiers, at different levels, had the muscle to make the best deals. Environmental management was the market, offering another chance to claim resources and improve free trade. In this context, the fluidity between public and private was a fertile space for capital, deals, plans, and the appearance of the economy itself.

The president's family and friends were exemplars of what every citizen was supposed to be doing; and their capital flowed out through transregional networks in small deals that complemented the large ones. Furthermore, this was a dynamic that supposedly sped up modernisation and development, the stated goal of the state. Secrets passed through personalistic ties encouraged speculation in which investments preceded contracts; for those tracking money and resources, an impatient anticipation emerged, speeding up the experience of time. A boom-time excitement was stimulated by the fluidity of deals, trickling down and then streaming between official coffers, foreign firms, and those-in-the-know. Rumours spread the excitement, and the wild men flocked to the frontier following or anticipating news of gold strikes and quick timber harvests, before the plantations rolled in. In this productive space, quick, erratic, anticipatory frontier time intensifies and spreads, ricocheting back and forth between centres and peripheries, and getting ahead of itself in death-defying leaps. Here alternative appearance-based scams—disciplined or wild—are born, and the only promise that must surely be kept is of fabulous, unearned wealth.

Roads That Empty the Territory

Between the tree plantations and the mountains are networks of more- and less-maintained logging roads, with their heavy cargoes of legal logs by day and illegal logs by night. For bosses and managers, the roads shrink and simplify the territory, making it quicker to get from here to there. For most everyone else, the logging roads expand landscape emptiness, separating off- and on-road sites and creating obstacles between once-connected forest places even as they speed the trip to town. The roads are also conduits for migrants, fugitives, and thieves, who expand both danger and wildness for everyone who lives or visits there.

Natural treasures themselves become fugitive in this landscape of movement and flight, just as once, people said, a man stumbled over a nugget of gold as big as a rice mortar and marked the place oh so carefully to come back later with help—but when he did, nothing was there. Masculine magic and charisma is required, for even safe in one's possession, treasures disappear. Thus every man on the road with a splinter of gaharu incense wood or a palmful of immature swallows' nests unwraps it from its plastic bag, shows it like a secret talisman, wraps it, stows its carefully in his pocket, chants the price, pulls it out again to rewrap it, trying thereby to stabilise its presence on his person. And how much more flighty are the incense trees and swallows themselves.

Take the swallows, for example. The saliva nests they build in limestone caves are the key ingredient of Chinese birds' nest soup and fetch startling prices even locally: a million and a half rupiah for 'a kilo of the white clean ones and 8,00,000 for the debris-filled black. In this area, they have long been associated with fugitive luck and danger. In the 1980s people told me that the only way to find birds' nests was to bring a freshly sacrificed human head to the spirits who could reveal them. Now, with armed men on the roads, the birds' erratic flight has intensified beyond the reach of headhunters, as have attempts to hold them in place. Where military men have found productive caves, they have posted guards and signs: 'This is the property of the army'. And so Meratus who consider themselves rightful traditional owners hurry to guard remaining caves, building their homes and clearing swiddens in the dark glens directly in front of the caves, never leaving them. Still, they are outmanoeuvred by the men on the roads, who come around with guns and flashlights and demand entry, peeling off the birds' nests long before they are fully built and indeed ensuring that the birds will not return. Quick harvesting leads to quicker harvesting, and nests the size of nail clippings are removed, depriving the birds of any place to raise their young. In this fugitive landscape, armed men are the best part of the law, and parodies of property appear. One Meratus man who built his house in front of a cave to guard it showed me the letter written by the most recent gang to have come by to rob the cave, which warned off future gangs on the principle of this group's precedence. My host got nothing, as did the swallows, who could only fly to other fugitive locations.

Men arm themselves with old war stories, and invulnerability magic from the 1958 rebellion has been revived, with its metaphors of penises as weapons and semen as spent bullets. As much as I tried to steer around the concerns of a simple ecofeminism, it was difficult not to conclude that an emergent masculinity fuelled this regionally spreading dynamic, with its ability to unite men across lines of local culture and religion in a competitively intensive virility. Men arouse each other on the roads with stories of women who will do anything (and then, he said, she tore off her bra). They work themselves and each other into a constant state of masculine anxiety, forever talking about deals and opportunities and prices in the sped-up time of the chase. They forget day-cycles, life-cycles, seasons. They call to and challenge each other to greater efforts.

Hiking the logging roads in the hot sun, I find it difficult to refuse a ride from the men in the truck. But crammed into the cab with the crew behind a windshield covered with stickers of busty naked ladies and my male Meratus friends stuck in the back with the water buffalo, fear hits me like an avalanche. Within 30 seconds, they are feeling my arms and legs and breasts, and I must concentrate on how to get them to let me off at the next crossroads, where I heave a sigh of relief that I made it out, again, this time. Yes, says a wizened Meratus friend, they grab your breasts even if you are a wrinkled old woman, they must have no eyes, and every woman longs and must learn to jump out of the truck. But a younger friend replies to my stories with bravado: why didn't you do it? weren't they handsome enough? I had heard similar bravado from young men when a peer was cowed by soldiers: if they had come at me, I would have shown them something! And indeed, one's only choices are to hide or to play. Women can be resourceful too, and prostitution brings new resources to the frontier. But this is a world made by an intensive, peculiar, exaggerated masculinity.

This is a masculinity that spreads and saturates itself with images and metaphors, amulets, stickers of naked women, stories based on the confusion between rape and wild sex. Its moving force is perhaps best seen in the imagistic effects of the 'water machine', the high-pressure hydraulic pump, small enough for one man to carry and connect to any local stream, but whose power in the spray emerging from the taut blue plastic piping can gouge a hole four feet deep into the land and thus expose the gravel underneath the clay, gravel mixed with which, perchance, small flakes or nuggets of gold can be found. What charismatic force! And what possibilities it unveils.

The water machine, introduced in this area around 1990, is the key technology of small-scale or 'wild' gold mining. It's much too expensive for an ordinary Meratus man, but networks of renting and share splitting, with borrowed funds and imagined profits split among more and more make it possible for many ambitious men to join a working group, or more aggressively yet, to bring the machine and a team upstream toward home. Nor are Meratus the only players. The miners, like the loggers, come from everywhere, building makeshift settlements along the logging roads with names like 'Kilometre 105 and a half'. At their excavations, they erect camps of bamboo platforms hung with plastic sheets; they have coffee pots, sugar, mackerel cans. But I know some of these people; they are Meratus farmer-foragers. I know they are perfectly capable of stopping anywhere in the forest and, in half an hour, building a cosy, rain-tight shelter of bamboo, palm leaves, or bark. I know, in other circumstances, they would carry rice; they would hunt and fish and gather wild fruits and vegetables and make a tasty meal. But here, surrounded by familiar forest, they observe the proprieties of rain-soaked plastic sheets and a nutrition of coffee and rancid fish. It feels like nothing so much as 'culture' in its most coercive, simplistic form: a way of life that draws us in, ready or not, sensible or not. Among the huddled mining shelters, men and women disagree. Women join the profit-sharing groups, panning the gravel with men until their own jealous menfolk arrive, sending them back to the village. The men attack the land with new vigour, sharing the washing with other women, and women sneak back to join the gold parties of strangers. But what is the result of all this passion? Despite obsessive attention to secrets and signs, much of the gravel exposed yields no metal at all; and when it does, the gold flakes are quickly spent in the extortionate prices of coffee, sugar, and cigarettes. No one I heard of had made much money; meanwhile, water machines broke and huge debts were accrued. Most strikingly, the land lay pock-marked and deeply eroded beyond recovery. Those trees that remained clung tottering by the tips of their roots, their bases airily exposed. Broken streams formed muddy pools; even grass was banished. 'They have ruined the land for many generations', said the old people. But perhaps it doesn't matter if the industrial tree plantations and their transmigrant labour force are coming anyway. Their mission is to make and restore degraded lands; why not get started?

Frontier Citizenship

Frontier men and resources, I have argued, are made in dynamics of intensification and proliferation. Confusions between legal and illegal, public and private, disciplined and wild are productive in sponsoring the emergence of men driven to profit, that is, entrepreneurs, as well as the natural objects conjured in their resourceful drives. These men and objects are contagious, recharging the landscape with wildness and virility. The frontier then appears to roll with its own momentum.

The frontier is a globally travelling project, but it requires localisation to come to life. I have tangled with this restless localisation by moving back and forth between the intense physicality of the frontier landscape, its guiding models, and its unplanned insights. Let me re-site it one more time in the hesitant emergence of frontier politics.

The frontier has been associated with distinctive political models of citizenship and culture. Most famously, frontier conditions are said to have made a freewheeling white male democracy in the new world. There is ongoing populist appeal here, not just in nostalgia for the US west, but more recently in respect for the independent miners of Brazil, who found their representatives and fought for their rights. Frontier fears of apocalypse have also stimulated models of protection: extractive reserves, indigenous reserves, nature reserves; each, at its best, produces an alliance among small collectors, native peoples, and forest advocates. Neither of these models made an easy entry into the cultural politics of Indonesia's New Order. In New Order models for the countryside, ethnic groups gained respect for cultural difference only with political submission: custom to keep farmers in their place. Yet frontier dynamics can unseat the obedience of custom to create a wider, wilder citizenship. Drawing men from everywhere, frontier culture can mobilise them both for and against each other.

A rhetoric of democracy is possible in official acts of protection of frontier culture, as when a governor of South Kalimantan once defended illegal logging as the livelihood of the people. Of course, this is a particular kind of democracy, in which women and indigenous residents—and, more firmly still, nature—are excluded. Then there is the question of race and ethnic violence, even genocide. This is the way frontier democracy has been made from below, at least historically. Thus far I have stressed transethnic collaboration, but this history alerts me to the lines and limits it also creates. Indeed, ethnic violence has come to fill out the Kalimantan frontier. In the mid-1990s, Dayaks mobilised in violent clashes with Madurese migrants in West Kalimantan. The year 2001 brought an eerily self-conscious echo in even more dramatic violence in Central Kalimantan; for a few days Dayak-Madurese clashes dominated international news. In the distorted lens of international journalism, one might imagine the scene as the return of the US Wild West—in its Hollywood version—with Dayaks as blood-thirsty savages scalping encroaching but civilised settlers. This is ridiculous parody; the clashes have their own political and cultural histories. Yet the emerging frontier is a place for the historical repetition of re-imagined savagery. Sometimes the army stages it; sometimes young men find themselves in its wild tropes. One's only choices are to hide or to play.

The reserve model has also attracted global attention. It arises in places where environmentalists are panicked by the possibility of total destruction; it argues that something must be saved. The most promising feature of this model is the mobilisation it has inspired, which brings the possibility of citizenship claims to those who never had them before: small collectors, tribes, trees. In Brazil, a moment of alliance between rubber tappers and Indians offered conservationists a strategy to save the forests. Yet in Indonesia, the alliance between frontiersmen and indigenous residents has only recruited the latter to the frontier. This has not been an alliance that saves forests.

Conservationists, in turn, have taken their pleas to corporations and the state, and these, indeed, have found some use for reserves. Resource companies support nature reserves because they cordon off a small area in exchange for permission to destroy the remaining countryside. Given the collusion between legal and illegal, disciplined and wild, and the new frontiersmen who come to complement development, corporate giants can rest assured they will get those reserves back, once appropriately degraded from below. Then too, in an age of natural simulation, it is never quite clear what is being preserved, what is degraded, and what is restored. The zones overlap and tease each other, and Indonesia now has national parks zoned as logging concessions. It is hard to know what one is seeing. Environmental activists say tree nurseries of hard-to-grow indigenous species are really cut-back natural forest, with young trees disguised as nursery seedlings. This, after all, is the salvage frontier. Meanwhile, maps contradict each other: a nature reserve sketched on one map is a production forest on another map, and a village territory on a third. A community forest designation is assigned to a treeless plain on which only dry stumps left by loggers recall living trees. The worst social coercions of conservation politics have been avoided in the areas I know best by not conserving anything at all.

In the late 1990s, the frontier began to spin out of control even from the perspective of capitalist investors and migrant entrepreneurs. In 1997, great fires broke out across Kalimantan, many of them set by the plantation companies who hoped to use this cheap method to clear their land. Since drought had been predicted due to the El Nino southern oscillation, the ministry of forests had warned the companies not to burn. But why consider regulation or prudence on the frontier? The fires spread beyond all expectation, destroying settlements and forests and forming a dangerous haze across south-east Asia. Then the financial crisis that had begun in Thailand spread to Indonesia and wiped out the promises of the New Order economic boom. Kalimantan villagers were most hurt by the crisis in the 'wildest' frontier areas, where subsistence agroforestry had already been threatened or ruined by corporate and immigrant expropriations as well as destruction of the forest landscape. Meanwhile, in West Kalimantan ethnic violence between indigenous Dayaks and immigrant Madurese flamed into a war. In 1998, demonstrations in Jakarta, together with international pressure, toppled the government. In the ensuing moment of political freedom, community groups, entrepreneurs, and gangsters seized corporate resource sites. Mines were occupied. Logging camps were destroyed. The wildness sponsored by the New Order had veered out of control.

With the passing of the New Order, great possibilities opened up. Finally, there was hope for an Indonesian democracy. Students and activists in Jakarta were jubilant. In Kalimantan, non-governmental organisations and activist alliances took a newly assertive role in advocating for the rights of rural communities. Yet the frontier sponsored by the New Order only proliferated, taking off in new leaps and bounds. The resources were surely there; who could ignore them? Decentralisation of resource rights, begun in 2000, pitted government officials at different levels against each other, such that the provincial governor and the regency assembly might fight continually over what forms of resource exploitation should be allowed—and who would get the proceeds. Meanwhile, regional groups within the military—no longer the tool of the central government—provoked ethnic violence and disorder. In 2001, Dayaks and Madurese became bloodily embroiled in Central Kalimantan. Still, hope rested on the possibility of new kinds of politics—as long as international powers allowed it. The US government decision in 2002 to rearm the Indonesian military for domestic surveillance in the 'war against terrorism' was a painful reminder of the international sponsorship of frontier violence. The frontier i s no neighbourhood storm. It gathers force from afar, entangling multiple local-to-global scales.

Back in California, I remember the frontier hero John Wayne—a man who wasn't even a Wild West cowboy but instead an actor who made his living pretending to be a Wild West cowboy. He never served in the military, but a congressional medal honoured him as the embodiment of American military heroism. Orange County has dedicated its airport to him, attracting visitors to the frontier—where adventure still leads to wealth, and a man with guns can stand tall. The frontier, like a film, can be played and replayed. That's resourcefulness on the salvage frontier.

8

Cultural Theory, Climate Change and Clumsiness

"They will never agree", said the 19th century wit, the Reverend Sidney Smith, when he saw two women shouting at each other from houses on opposite sides of an Edinburgh street, "they are arguing from different premises". Cultural theorists [e.g. Adams 1995:50 and Douglas and Wildavsky 1982:174] like to use this story as a way of getting to grips with the disputes that characterise environmental policy. The different premises, in these disputes, concern human and physical nature, and cultural theory maps them in terms of a fourfold typology of forms of social solidarity (figure). Two of these solidarities—individualism and hierarchy—have long been familiar to social scientists; they are usually referred to as markets and hierarchies [e g Williamson 1975 and Lindblom 1977]. The theory's novelty lies in its addition of the other two solidarities and in its making explicit the different premises—the different social constructions of nature, physical and human—that sustain these four fundamental arrangements for the promotion of social transactions. Hierarchies institute status differences (asymmetrical transactions) and, by requiring forms of behaviour appropriate to those of differing rank and station (accountability), set all sorts of limits on competition. Markets—the transactional arrangements that accompany individualism—do the diametrical opposite; they institute equality of opportunity (symmetrical transactions) and promote competition (no accountability, as in 'If I don't do it someone else will'). The other two permutations: symmetrical transactions with accountability (labelled egalitarianism in the cultural theory scheme), and asymmetrical transactions without accountability (labelled fatalism in the cultural theory scheme) tend to be ignored by social science in general and by policy science in particular. This, for instance, was evidently the case with the enormous Brent Spar oil storage structure, the deep ocean disposal of which was proposed by the market actor—Shell—and approved by the hierarchical actor—the British government's regulatory agency. Had there been only markets and hierarchies the Brent Spar would now be mouldering in its watery grave, but of course it isn't! Another actor—Greenpeace—from a third form of solidarity (egalitarianism) forced its way in, at the 11th hour, by audaciously, and very publicly, landing a helicopter on the structure as it was being towed out into the Atlantic. The disposal plans were abruptly abandoned by Shell (motorists, particularly in Germany, having stopped buying its petrol) and the British government was left with egg all over its face (John Major, the prime minister at the time, called Shell's senior management 'wimps'). Shell then entered into lengthy negotiations with Greenpeace, and the Brent Spar has now been cut up into cylindrical sections to help form a ferry terminal in Norway. Those British citizens who managed to remain ignorant of the whole affair (and they were many), or who found themselves totally convinced by whoever they happened to have last seen arguing their case on television, were evidently bound into none of these 'active' solidarities—individualism, hierarchy or egalitarianism—and constituted a fourth and rather 'inactive' solidarity—fatalism—assuring one another either that 'ignorance is bliss' or that 'nothing we could do would make any difference, anyway'.

So cultural theory, by doubling-up from two solidarities to four, is able to make sense—predictive sense—of something that must always remain beyond the explanatory reach—a perennial source of surprise—of those who have equipped themselves with the conventional social science wisdom. That, I would argue, is why this theory merits our attention.

The Four-fold Solidarities

For upholders of the individualist solidarity, nature is benign and resilient—able to recover from any exploitation (hence the iconic myth of nature: a ball that, no matter how profoundly disturbed, always returns to stability)—and man is inherently self-seeking and atomistic. Trial and error, in self-organising ego-focused networks (markets), is the way to go, with Adam Smith's invisible hand ensuring that people only do well when others also benefit. Individualists, in consequence, trust others until they give them reason not to and then retaliate in kind (the winning 'tit for tat' strategy in the iterated Prisoner's Dilemma game [Rapoport 1985]). They see it as only fair that (as in the joint stock company) those who put most in get most out. Managing institutions that work 'with the grain of the market' (getting rid of environmentally harmful subsidies, for instance) are what are needed.

Nature, for those who bind themselves into the egalitarian solidarity, is almost the exact opposite (hence the ball on the upturned basin)—fragile, intricately interconnected and ephemeral—and man is essentially caring and sharing (until corrupted by coercive and inegalitarian institutions: markets and hierarchies).

We must all tread lightly on the Earth, and it is not enough that people start off equal; they must end up equal as well—equality of result. Trust and levelling go hand-in-hand, and institutions that distribute unequally are distrusted. Voluntary simplicity is the only solution to our environmental problems, with the 'precautionary principle' being strictly enforced on those who are tempted not to share the simple life.

The world, in the hierarchical solidarity, is controllable. Nature is stable until pushed beyond discoverable limits (hence the two humps), and man is malleable: deeply flawed but redeemable by firm, long-lasting and trustworthy institutions. Fair distribution is by rank and station or, in the modern context, by need (with the level of need being determined by expert and dispassionate authority). Environmental management requires certified experts (to determine the precise locations of nature's limits) and statutory regulation (to ensure that all economic activity is then kept within those limits).

Fatalist actors (or perhaps we should say non-actors, since their voice is seldom heard in policy debates; if it was they wouldn't be fatalistic!) find neither rhyme nor reason in nature, and know that man is fickle and untrustworthy. Fairness, in consequence, is not to be found in this life, and there is no possibility of effecting change for the better. 'Defect first'—the winning strategy in the one-off Prisoner's Dilemma—makes sense here, given the unreliability of communication and the permanent absence of prior acts of good faith. With no way of ever getting in sync with nature (push the ball this way or that and the feedback is everywhere the same), or of building trust with others, the fatalist's world (unlike those of the other three solidarities) is one in which learning is impossible. 'Why bother?' therefore, is the rational management response.

These solidarities, in varying strengths and patterns of pair-wise alliance, are clearly discernible almost anywhere you care to look: in debates over water engineering in south Asia [Gyawali 2001]; in the international fora where delegates struggle to do something about climate change [Thompson, Rayner and Ney 1998; Verweij 2001]; in the different ways international regimes cope with trans-boundary risks such as water pollution [Verweij 2000] and municipalities go about the business of transport planning [Hendriks 1994]; in the various ways households set about making ends meet [Dake and Thompson 1999]; in the different diagnoses of the pensions crisis in countries with ageing populations [Ney 1997]; and in the different panaceas that are variously championed and rejected by theorists of public administration [Hood 1998], to mention but a few.

In all these examples we find that each solidarity, in creating a context that is shaped by its distinctive premises, generates a storyline that inevitably contradicts those that are generated by the other solidarities. Yet, since each distils certain elements of experience and wisdom that are missed by the others, and since each provides a clear expression of the way in which a significant portion of the populace feels we should live with one another and with nature, it is important that they all be taken some sort of account of in the policy process. That, in essence, is the case for clumsiness, and I can now expand it with the help of a worked example: climate change.

Contested Terrain of Climate Change

The global climate change debate, of course, is still going on, but an analysis of that debate in the mid-1990s provides us with a convenient point of entry: three policy stories (three, because the fatalist solidarity has no voice: if it had it would not be fatalistic). Each policy story provides a setting (the basic assumptions), a villain (the policy problem), heroes (policy protagonists), and, of course, a moral (the policy solution). Depending on the socio-institutional context of the particular policy actor, each story emphasises different aspects of the climate change issue. What is more, each story defines itself in contradistinction to the other policy stories.

Profligacy: An Egalitarian Story

This story begins by pointing to the profligate consumption and production patterns of the north as the fundamental cause of global climate change. Rich industrialised countries, so the argument goes, are recklessly pillaging the world's resources with little regard to the well-being of either the planet or the people of its poorer regions. Global climate change is more than an issue that is amenable to quick technical fixes; it is a fundamentally moral and ethical issue. The setting for this story is a world in which everything is intricately connected to everything else: Nature Ephemeral (figure). Whether this concerns human society or the natural world, this story urges us to think of Planet Earth as a single living entity. Environmental degradation, then, is also an attack on human well-being. Humans, so the argument goes, have, until now, successfully deluded themselves that they can live apart from the natural environment. In reality, however, there is no place for humans outside nature and thus no particular reason for considering humans as superior to nature. In short, this story is set in an ecocentric world.

The villain, in the profligacy story, is the fundamentally inequitable structure of advanced industrial society. In particular, the profit motive and the obsession with economic growth—the driving forces of global capitalism—have not only brought us to the brink of ecological disaster; they have also distorted our understanding of both the natural and the social world. Global commerce and the advertising industry lead us to desire environmentally unsustainable products (bottled water, fast cars, or high protein foods, for example) while our real human needs (living in harmony with nature and with each other: the egalitarian's social construction of human nature) go unfulfilled. What is more, advanced capitalism distributes the spoils of global commerce highly inequitably. This is true within countries (the increasing gap between the rich classes and the poor classes) and among countries (the increasing gap between the affluent countries of the north and the destitute countries of the south). In short, prevailing structural inequalities have led to increasingly unsustainable patterns of consumption and production.

Since everything is connected to everything else, this story continues, we cannot properly understand environmental degradation unless we see it as a symptom of this wider social malaise. The way humans pollute, degrade and destroy the natural world is merely a very visible indicator for the way they treat each other and particularly the weaker members of society. The logic that allows us to fell thousands of square kilometres of rainforests, to dump toxins in waterways, or pollute the air is precisely the same logic that produces racism, misogyny and xenophobia. Tackling one problem inevitably implies tackling all the others.

The heroes of the profligacy story are those organisations and individuals who have managed to see through the chimera of progress in advanced industrial society. They are those groups and persons that understand that the fate of humans is inextricably linked to the fate of Planet Earth. The heroes understand that, in order to halt environmental degradation, we have to address the fundamental global inequities. In short, the heroes of the profligacy policy argument are those organisations of protest such as, most prominently, Greenpeace or Friends of the Earth. These organisations, I need hardly point out, are strongly biased towards the egalitarian social solidarity.

What, then, is the moral of the profligacy story? Its proponents point to a number of solutions. In terms of immediate policy, the profligacy tale urges us to adopt the precautionary principle in all cases: unless policy actors can prove that a particular activity is innocuous to the environment, they should refrain from it. The underlying idea here is that the environment is precariously balanced on the brink of a precipice. The story further calls for drastic cuts in carbon dioxide emissions; since the industrialised north produces most of these emissions, the onus is on advanced capitalist states to take action. Of course, this policy argument calls for a total and complete ban on chlorofluorocarbons.

Yet none of these measures, the story continues, is likely to be fruitful on its own. In order to really tackle the problem of global climate change those in the affluent north will have to fundamentally reform their political institutions and their unsustainable lifestyles. Rather than professionalised bureaucracies and huge centralised administrations, the advocates of the profligacy story suggest we decentralise decision-making down to the grass roots level. Rather than continuing to produce ever-increasing amounts of waste, we should aim at conserving the fragile natural resources we have: we should, in a word, move from the idea of a waste society to the concept of a conserve. society. Only then can we meet real human needs. What are real human needs? Simple, they are the needs of Planet Earth.

Population: A Hierarchist Story

This policy argument tells a story of uncontrolled population growth in the poorer regions of the world. Rapidly increasing population in the south, this story argues, is placing local and global ecosystems under pressures that are fast becoming dangerously uncontrollable: more people mean more resource consumption which inevitably leads to environmental degradation. The setting of the population policy story differs slightly, but significantly, from the settings in the other two diagnoses. Like the protagonists of the profligacy story, the population policy argument maintains that global climate change is a moral issue. Human beings, due to their singular position in the natural world, are the custodians of Planet Earth; since civilisation and technological progress have allowed us to understand the natural world more than other species, we have a moral obligation to apply this knowledge wisely. Unlike the profligacy story, the population tale assumes that humans have a special status outside natural processes. The population story, like that of the proponents of the pricing argument (see next story), contends that human actions are rational. However, unlike the pricing argument, the population story tells us the sum of individual rational actions can lead to irrational and detrimental outcomes. The population story, then, is set in a world that needs rational management in order to become sustainable. Yet, while the motive of rational management is an ethical duty to preserve the planet, the means of management are technical. Economic growth, and the socio-economic system that underpins that growth, are necessary components in any global climate change policy response. However, economic growth in itself is no solution: it must be tempered, directed, and balanced by the careful application of knowledge and judgment.

The villain in the population tale is uncontrolled population growth. Since each individual has a fixed set of basic human needs (such as food, shelter, security, etc) and these needs are then standardised at every level of socio-economic development (the hierarchist's social construction of human nature), population increase, other things being equal, must lead to an increase in the aggregate demand for resources. Humans, the story insists, satisfy their basic human needs by consuming resources. It follows that population growth must lead to an increase in resource consumption:

more people will produce more carbon dioxide to satisfy their basic needs. (Though this can be mitigated, in the longer term, by carefully planned and managed changes in technology: away from fossil fuels and towards renewables or nuclear—fission and eventually fusion.) Given the limited nature of most resources, population growth must invariably lead to overconsumption and degradation of natural resources.

The heroes of the population story are those institutions with both the organisational capacities (that is, the technical knowledge) and the 'right' sense of moral responsibility. In short, the global climate change issue should be left to experts situated in large-scale, well-organised administrations (the Intergovernmental Panel on Climate Change (IPCC), for instance). In terms of our typology of ways of organising, the population story emerges from hierarchically structured institutions.

The moral of the population story is to rationally control population growth. In particular, this means the introduction of family planning and education in the countries most likely to suffer from rapid population growth. Here, the onus for action is quite clearly on the countries of the south. Rapid population growth has eroded societal management capacities; if we are to tackle the global climate change issue we must first establish the proper organisational preconditions.

Prices: An Individualist Story

This story locates the causes of global climate change in the relative prices of natural resources. Historically, prices have poorly reflected the underlying economic scarcities; the result, plain for all to see, is a relative over-consumption of natural resources.

The setting of the prices tale is the world of markets and economic growth. Unlike the profligacy story, the prices diagnosis sees no reason to muddy the conceptual waters with extraneous considerations of social equality. Yes, it says, global climate change is an important issue, but it is an issue that is amenable to precise analytical treatment. It is, in short, a technical issue to which we can apply a technical discourse. Economic growth, far from being a problem, is the sole source of salvation from environmental degradation. Environmental protection, the proponents of this policy argument contend, is a very costly business. In order, then, to be able to foot the huge bill for adjusting to a more sustainable economy, societies will have to command sufficient funds. These funds, in turn, will not materialise from thin air: only economic growth can provide the necessary resources to tackle the expensive task of greening the economy.

In sum, the prices tale takes place in a world determined by the invisible hand. Here, people know and can precisely rank their preferences (the individualist's social construction of human nature). In the prices story, individual pursuit of rational self-interest (economic utility) leads, as if by magic (though economists such as Hayek prefer to call it 'self-organisation'), to the optimal allocation of resources. If market forces are allowed to operate as they should then resource prices will accurately reflect underlying scarcities; the price mechanism then keeps environment-degrading consumption in check. However, if someone (usually the misguided policy-maker) meddles with market forces, prices cannot reflect real scarcities; this gives rise to incentives for rational economic actors to over- or under-consume a particular resource.

The villain in the prices story is misguided economic policy. Barriers to international trade, subsidies to inefficient national industries, as well as price and wage floors, introduce distortions to the self-regulatory powers of the market. These distortions have historically led markets to place a monetary value on natural resources that belies the true market value. The result, the protagonists of this policy argument maintain, has been wholesale over-consumption and degradation of the natural world. The heroes of the prices story are those institutions that understand the economics of resource consumption. In the global climate change debate, these institutions comprise players such as the Global Climate Coalition and trans-national energy companies. In terms of the cultural theory typology, the heroes of this story are those institutions that are strongly permeated by the individualist solidarity (The Economist, for instance, and think-tanks such as Britain's Institute of Economic Affairs and the US's Competitive Enterprise Institute).

The moral of the prices story is as simple as its prognosis; in order to successfully face the challenge of global climate change we have to 'get the prices right'. Unlike the profligacy story, the prices tale sees no necessity to restructure existing institutions. If it is the distortions of global, national and regional market mechanisms that undervalue natural resources then any climate change policy that fails to remove these distortions is 'fundamentally flawed'. Policy responses must work 'with the market'. Here, concrete policy proposals consist of both general measures, such as the liberalisation of global trade, as well as more specific measures, such as carbon taxes or tradable emission permits (with a strong preference for the latter, taxes being seen as more likely to distort the market).

Consequently, it is only by teasing out these sorts of policy arguments, and their diverse adherents, that we can understand the social constructions of needs and resources; how they are generated, how they are reproduced and transformed, and how they shape the policy process. This understanding has some important implications.

The three stories tell plausible but conflicting tales of climate change. All three tales use reason and logic to argue their points. None of the tales is 'wrong', in the sense of being implausible or incredible. Yet, at the same time, none of the stories is completely 'right'; each argument focuses on those aspects of climate change for which there is a suitable solution cast within the terms of a particular form of organisation.

These three policy discourses are not reducible to one another. No one of the policy arguments is a close substitute for the others. Nor are any of the stories' proponents ever likely to agree on the fundamental causes of and solutions to the global climate change issue. And, since these stories implicitly convey a normative argument, namely, that of the good life (either in egalitarian enclaves, in hierarchies, or in markets), they are curiously immune to enlightenment by 'scientific' facts; we cannot, in any scientific sense, prove or falsify policy stories.

These stories also define what sort of evidence counts as a legitimate fact and what type of knowledge is credible. The profligacy story discounts economic theory as the obfuscation of social inequalities and dismisses rational management as the reification of social relations. The tale of prices views holistic eco-centrism as amateur pop-science and pours scorn on the naive belief in benign control. Last, the population story rejects laissez-faire economic theory as dangerously unrealistic and questions the scientific foundations of more holistic approaches.

This leaves us with a dynamic, plural and argumentative system of policy-definition and policy-framing that policy-makers can ignore only at their cost, for two reasons. First, each policy story, as we have seen, thematises a pertinent aspect of the climate change debate; very few would argue that northern consumption habits, population growth or distorted prices have no impact on global climate change at all. However, as we have seen, each story places a different emphasis on each aspect. Any global climate change policy, then, based on only one or two of these stories, will merely provide a response to a specific aspect of the global climate change problem. It will, in short, provide a partially effective response. Second, and more significantly, each of the stories represents a political voice in the policy process. Ignoring any of these voices means excluding them from policy-making. Within democratic polities, this inevitably leads to a loss of legitimacy. What is more, in democracies, dissenting voices will eventually force their way into the policy process (as we have seen for instance, with the Brent Spar and, more recently, with the World Trade Organisation in Seattle and Prague and the G8 riots in Genoa). Neither the cost of acrimonious and vicious political conflict, nor the loss of public trust experienced by those who (perhaps inadvertently, perhaps not) suppress dissenting voices, are particularly attractive. The former often leads to policy deadlock; the latter may well result in a legitimacy crisis in the polity as a whole.

So these three policy stories have important implications, not just for global climate change policy-making, but (and this is where the range of applications I mentioned earlier comes back into the picture) for policy, and for risk management, generally. Endemic conflict: In a policy process where politics matters (that is, in any policy process) there will always be at least three divergent but plausible stories that frame the issue, define the problem, and suggest solutions. Thus conflict in policy-making processes is endemic, inevitable, and desirable, rather than pathological, curable or deviant. Any policy process that does not take this into account does so at the risk of losing political legitimacy.

Plural policy responses: We have seen that each story tells a plausible, but selective, story. Any policy response modelled solely in terms of just one or two of these tales will be, at best, partial and, at worst, irrelevant.

Quality of communication: Since policy-making is inherently conflictual, and since effective policy responses depend on the participation of all three voices, policy outcomes crucially depend on the quality of the communication within the debate. A policy debate that can harness the inherent communicative and argumentative conflict between different story-tellers will profit most from the potentially constructive interaction between different proponents. Conversely, a policy debate in which all three positions are sharply polarised will probably lead to policy deadlock. This is a structural argument that concerns the implicit and explicit 'rules' that govern policy deliberation in a polity. If the 'rules of the game' permit or even force policy actors to take seriously different types of stories, then what Sabatier and Jenkins-Smith call 'policy-oriented learning' can take place. If this is not the case, then the policy debate will be an unconstructive dialogue of the deaf [Sabatier and Jenkins-Smith 1993].

Summarising all of the above, we have at one extreme an unresponsive monologue and at the other a shouting match amongst the totally deaf. Between these extremes we occasionally find a vibrant multivocality in which each voice puts its view as persuasively as possible, sensitive to the knowledge that others are likely to disagree, and acknowledging a responsibility to listen to what the others are saying. This is the condition—clumsiness—we must strive

.for if we value democracy or, as is the case with many regulatory agencies, we are mandated to develop and implement policy on behalf of a democracy. Getting there and staying there is, of course, not easy.

At the monologue end of the spectrum the policy process is seductively elegant and reassuringly free (it would seem) from the defiling intrusion of politics. Here we find the mindset characterised by single-metric rationality. At the other extreme we wallow in the incoherence of complete relativism. The cultural theory typology presented here suggests that between these extremes there is the possibility of constructive dialogue. It will often be a noisy, discordant, contradictory dialogue, but this is the clumsy beast that democratic policy-makers and regulators must seek to harness and ride.

Making Ourselves Clumsy

The term 'clumsy institution' was coined by Michael Schapiro (1988) as a way of escaping from the idea that, when we are faced with contradictory definitions of problem and solution, we must choose one and reject the rest. Clumsy institutions, we can say, now that we have the cultural theory typology, are those institutional arrangements in which none of the voices—the hierarchist's calling for 'wise guidance and careful stewardship', the individualist's urging us to 'get the prices right', the egalitarian's insisting that we need 'a whole new relationship with nature', and the fatalist's asking 'why bother?'—is excluded, and in which the contestation is harnessed to constructive, if noisy, argumentation.

Clumsiness emerges as preferable to elegance (optimising around just one of the definitions of the problem and, in the process, silencing the other voices) once we realise that what looks like irreconcilable contradiction is. in fact, essential contestation. Moreover, since each voice usually argues that its solution will strengthen democracy, whilst those being urged by the others will weaken it, democracy too becomes an essentially contested concept: a concept which, following Gallic (1955), can never be pinned down in a single way but can be clarified only through regular argument; that is, through discourse.

Each solidarity, therefore, has its own social construction of democracy: its 'model' [Hendriks and Zourides 1999] or 'image' [Jensen 1999]. Clumsiness, in consequence, has normative implications that link policy, technology and democracy in ways that mainstream political science has disregarded [see, for instance, Ney and Thompson 1999 and Tranvik, Thompson and Selle 2001].5 If we haven't got all the models of democracy—clearly voiced and engaged with one another in the public sphere—then, so the normative argument goes, we haven't got democracy!

Hierarchists, siding with Plato and his philosopher-king, subscribe to the guardian model, in which it is only right that those with superior insight and virtue should do their trustee-like duty and make all the decisions. Democracy should be indirect, majoritarian and representative, with the political class being given primacy over public affairs on the basis of popular elections every few years.

Individualists see self-determination as crucial and dislike both paternalism and majoritarianism (which, they point out, can result in even quite large minorities being prevented from 'carrying out their plans'). Theirs is a protective model and, siding with Locke, they see government's raison d'etre as 'the protection of life, liberty and estate'.

Egalitarians are more with Rousseau, rejecting deference and seeing self-interest as something to be reined in, not amplified. They plump for the participatory model, in which the equal right to self-development is what matters, and this means that choice should be by broad and direct participation, ideally in a small-scale, face-to-face way and at a single level: the grass roots.

Fatalists, too, have their distinctive, and characteristically unenthusiastic, model: a non-model, really. Despite the other solidarities' fine words about public goods, private goods and common-pool goods, fatalists know that these are all really club goods, from which they have been excluded. Hence struggling to define who the decision-maker should be is a waste of effort. It does not matter who you vote for, fatalists assure one another, the government always gets in.

From the reflexive vantage point that is afforded us by

our fourfold typology (figure), and with the benefit of hindsight, it can be seen that many of our public institutions—Britain's former ministry of agriculture, fisheries and food, the WTO, the IPCC, and most national overseas aid agencies, to mention but a few—are insufficiently clumsy and, in consequence, erosive of democracy. Most policy tools (all single metrics such as cost-benefit analysis, probabilistic risk assessment, quality-adjusted life years, general equilibrium modelling) and policy precepts (the insistence on a single agreed definition of the problem, the clear separation of facts and values, and the focus on optimisation) are similarly flawed.

Bibliography

Andersen, Perry (2002): —'Force and Consent', *New Left Review* 17: 5-30.

Appadurai, Arjun (1986): *The Social Life of Things: Commodities in Cultural Perspective,* Cambridge University Press, Cambridge.

"Development" in Zimbabwe's Eastern Highlands'. *American Ethnologist,* (forthcoming b): 'The Dream Machine: The Model Development Project and the Remaking of the State' in Amita Baviskar (ed) *Waterscapes: The Cultural Politics of a Natural Resource.*

Gujarat Ecology Commission (1994): Current Ecological Status of Kachchh.

Moore, Donald S., Anand Pandian and Jake Kosek (2003): *The Cultural Action in South India,* Oxford University Press, Delhi.

Peluso, Nancy and Michael Watts (eds) (2001): *Violent Environments, the 'Improvement' of the World,* Yale University Press, New Haven.

Balla, Balint (1980) 'Ressourcenknappheit und Soziales Handeln' in Friedrich Rapp (ed), Nahirverslaendnis und Soziales Handeln, Wilhelm Fink.

Brosius, J. Peter (1999): 'Analyses and Interventions: Anthropological Engagements with Environmentalism', *Current Anthropology,* 40 (3): 277-309.

Coronil, Fernando (1997): *The Magical State: Nature, Money, and Modernity,* California Press, Berkeley.

Drayton, Richard (2000): *Nature's Government: Science, Imperial Britain,* Cambridge University Press, Cambridge.

Saberwal, Vasant and Mahesh Rangarajan (eds) (2003): *Battles over Nature: 19th Century British Liberal Thought,* University of Chicago Press, Chicago.

Mitchell, Timothy (2002): *Rule of Experts: Egypt, Techno-Politics and Colonial Eastern India,* Stanford University Press, Stanford.

Watts, Michael (2001): *Petro-Violence: Community, Extraction, and Political Colonialism and Culture,* University of Michigan Press, Ann Arbor.

Malkki, Liisa (1992): 'National Geographic: The Rooting of Peoples and Cultural Anthropology, 7 (1): 24-44.

Mehta, Uday Singh (1999): *Liberalism and Empire: A Study in Nineteenth Century Britain.*

D. Parkin (eds) *Bush Base, Forest Farm: Culture, Environment and Development,* Routledge, New York.

Sivaramakrishnan, K (2003): *Conservation Crossroads: Indian Wildlife at Difference,* Duke University Press, Durham.

Mosse, David (2003): 'The Rule of Water: Statecraft, Ecology, and Collective Ecology of a Mythic Commodity'.

Williams, Raymond (1976): *Keywords: A Vocabulary of Culture and Society.*

Herman, Edward and Noam Chomsky (1994): *Manufacturing Consent.*

Raju, K.C. B. (1995): 'Strategies to Combat Mechanisms and Long-Term Solutions to Drought', *Social Action.*

Douglas, M. and A. Wildavsky (1982): *Risk and Culture,* University of Chicago Press, Chicago.

Fuller, C.J. and Veronique Benei (2000): *The Everyday State and Society of Water in Western India,* Orient Longman, India.

Morse, B and Thofflas-Jierger (1992): *Sardar Sarovar: Report of the over India's Narmada River.* ME Sharpe.

Armonk, Gleick, P.H. (1993): *Water in Crisis: A Guide to the World's Fresh Water.*

Olsen, W. (1987): 'Manmade Drought in Rayalaseema', *Economic and Political Weekly.*

Peasant Resistance in the Himalaya, Oxford University Press, Delhi.

PMiller (eds) *The Foucault Effect: Studies in Governmentalhy.*

Political Economy of the Mass Media, Pantheon Books, New York.

Herzfeld, Michael (1997): *Cultural Intimacy: Social Poetics in the Nation.*

Kutch Development Forum (1993): *A Demand for Review of Water Allocation.*

Ludden, David (1992): 'India's Development Regime' in N.B. Dirks (ed) r, Amita (forthcoming a): 'Red in Tooth and Claw?: Searching for Class in Struggles over Nature' in Raka Ray and Mary Katzenstein (eds) *Rethinking Class and Poverty: Social Movements in India in a Transnational Age,* Reason, Polity Press, Cambridge.

Review Group on Narmada, KDF, Bombay.

Mehta, Lyla (2000): 'Drought Diagnosis: Dryland Blindness of Planners', Rural Development Centre, Uppsala.

Fisher. William (ed) (1995): *Towards Sitstainable Development.*

Science and the Politics of Conservation, Permanent Black, Delhi.

Said, Edward W (1993): *Culture and Imperialism,* Knopf, New York.

Shaw, Rosalind (1992): "Nature', 'Culture' and Disasters' in E Croll, *Science and the Politics of Conservation,* Permanent Black, Delhi.

Falkenmark, M., J. Lundquist and C. Widstrand (1990): 'Coping with Water the Analysisot Environmental Problems', Progress in Human Geography, the Grasslands of Kachchh District, Gujarat State, India.

Bourdieu, Pierre (1998): 'The Economy of Symbolic Goods',

Practical the Nicaraguan State, 1894-1987, Stanford University Press, Stanford.

Herman, E.S. and Noam Chomsky (1988): *Manufacturing Consent: The Territorialisation of National Identity among Scholars and Refugees.*

Use and Abuse of Nature in Contemporary India, Penguin, New Delhi.

Desai, Bharat (1995): `Narmada Dam will not Help Save Kutch'.